The Illustrator 6 Wow! Book

Sharon Steuer

Editor: Gary Pfitzer
Book Designer: Barbara Sudick
Revisions Co-author: Mordy Golding

The Illustrator 6 Wow! Book
Sharon Steuer

Peachpit Press
2414 Sixth Street
Berkeley, CA 94710
510 548-4393
800 283-9444
510 548-5991 fax
Find us on the World Wide Web at:
http://www.peachpit.com

Peachpit Press is a division of Addison Wesley Longman.

Copyright © 1995, 1996 by Sharon Steuer
Editor: Gary Pfitzer
Book design: Barbara Sudick
Cover design: Barbara Sudick
Cover illustration: Sharon Steuer
Revisions Co-author: Mordy Golding
Series Editor: Linnea Dayton

ISBN 0–201–88664–2

0 9 8 7 6 5 4 3 2 1

Printed and bound in the United States of America.

Contents

* See the Wow! disk's Plug-ins folder and Other Programs folder
for related demos and free samples.

Important: **Read me first!**

What's new in Illustrator 6?

When upgrading to a new version of a program, many people prefer to learn about all the new features at once. Therefore, in addition to the tips, tricks and techniques found within the pages of this book, on the *Wow!* disk you'll find a special folder called *What's New in Illustrator 6?* This folder contains feature-by-feature summaries and new step-by-step lessons designed to introduce you to Illustrator 6. Within the text of the book, look for the ❻ to indicate when additional information about a specific new feature can be found in the *What's New in Illustrator 6?* folder.

Additional Illustrator training

Learning is often accelerated by taking a good class; the *Training* folder on the *Wow!* disk includes a suggested *Illustrator Wow!* course curriculum and a listing of facilities offering classes in Illustrator. Try the animated tutorials on the *Adobe Illustrator CD*, and the *Zen Lessons* on the *Wow!* disk that supplement *Chapter 2*. Additional suggested reading can be found in the *Publications* appendix.

This book has been designed to help you harness the enormous power of Adobe Illustrator by providing you with hundreds of pages of useful production techniques, timesaving tips and beautiful art generously shared by *Illustrator Wow!* artists nationwide. Whether you're a recent convert to Illustrator, or one of the thousands of Illustrator experts who haven't had the time to learn the newer features, this book is for you. All techniques were kept deliberately short to allow you to squeeze in a lesson or two between clients, and to encourage the use of this book within the confines of a supervised classroom.

In order to keep the content in this book tantalizing to everyone—from novice to expert—I've assumed a reasonable level of competence with basic Macintosh concepts such as opening and saving files, launching applications, copying objects to the clipboard, and doing basic mouse operations. I've also assumed that you've completed the *Adobe Illustrator Tutorial*, and understand conceptually the basic functionality of the tools.

I'd love to tell you that you can learn Adobe Illustrator by flipping through the pages of this book, but the reality is, there is no substitute for practice. The good news is, the more you work with Illustrator, the more features you'll be able to integrate into your creative process.

Use this book as a reference, a guide for special techniques, or just a source of inspiration. After you've read this book, read it again, and you'll undoubtedly learn something you missed the first time. As I hope you'll discover, the more experienced you become with Adobe Illustrator, the easier it will be to assimilate all the new information and inspiration you'll find in this book. Happy Illustrating!

Sharon Steuer

How to use this book...

Before you do anything else, read the *Glossary* found inside the back cover. The *Glossary* provides definitions for the terms used throughout *The Illustrator 6 Wow! Book* (such as ⌘ = the Command key, and what "grab" means). In addition to terms defined in the *Glossary*, you'll find six kinds of information woven throughout this book—all of it up-to-date for Illustrator 6: **Basics**, **Tips**, **Exercises**, **Techniques**, **Galleries** and **References**.

1 Basics. *Chapter 1: Illustrator Basics* and *Chapter 2: The Zen of Illustrator* qualify as full-blown chapters on basics and are packed with information that distills and supplements your Adobe Illustrator manuals and disks. Every chapter starts with a general overview of the basics. Although these sections have been designed so that advanced users of Illustrator can move quickly through them, I strongly suggest that the rest of you read them very carefully. Please keep in mind that this book serves as a supplement to, not a substitute for, your Adobe Illustrator *User Guides* and CD-ROM.

2 Tips. Look to the information in the gray boxes for hands-on tips that can help you work more efficiently. Usually you can find tips alongside related textual information, but if you are in too impatient a mood to read a section in depth, you might just want to flip through, looking for tips that are of interest to you. The red arrows ➞, red outlines and red text found in tips (and sometimes with artwork) have been added to emphasize or further explain a concept or technique. Look for the ⑥ symbol throughout the text to indicate that more information about this feature can be found on the *Wow!* disk.

3 Exercises. (Not for the faint of heart.) I have included intermediate-level, step-by-step exercises to help you make the transition to Illustrator technician extraordinaire.

2 **Tip boxes and ⑥ symbols**
Look for these boxes to find Tips. Look for the ⑥ symbol to indicate that more information about a feature can be found in the *What's New in Illustrator 6?* folder on the *Wow!* disk. For easier access, copy the ⑥ folder to your hard disk.

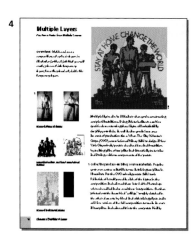

4

5

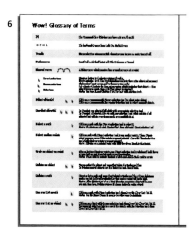

6

Chapter 2: *The Zen of Illustrator* and the *Zen Lessons* on the *Wow!* disk are dedicated to helping you master the mechanics, and the soul, of Illustrator. Take these lessons in small doses, in order, and at a relaxed pace.

4 Techniques. In these sections, you'll find step-by-step techniques based on work from dozens of *Illustrator Wow!* artists. Each *Wow!* technique focuses on one aspect of how an image was created. I will often refer you to different *Wow!* chapters, or to a specific page where a technique is introduced to give you the opportunity to explore a briefly-covered function in more depth. Feel free to start with almost any chapter, but, since each technique builds on previously explained ones, try to follow the techniques within each chapter sequentially. Some chapters will conclude with an **Advanced Technique**, which assumes that you have assimilated all of the techniques found throughout the chapter. *Chapter 8: Masks & Special Effects* is an entire chapter of advanced tips and techniques. Find special Illustrator 6 techniques in the *What's New in Illustrator 6?* folder (❻) on the *Wow!* disk.

5 Galleries. The gallery pages consist of images related to a technique demonstrated nearby. Each gallery piece is accompanied by a description of how the artist created that image, and may include steps showing the progression of a technique detailed elsewhere in the chapter. The final chapter, *Chapter 9: Illustrator & Other Programs*, consists almost entirely of gallery pages devoted to Illustrator working in combination with other programs.

6 References. *Technical Notes, Resources, Publications* and *Artists* appendixes, and a *General Index* can be found in the back of this book. In addition, I will sometimes direct you to the *User Guide* when referring to specific information which is already well-documented in either the *Adobe Illustrator User Guide* or the *Getting Started* supplement. And remember, ❻ indicates that more information on this new feature is found on the *Wow!* disk.

Illustrator Basics

1

Illustrator Basics

Introduction...

Why you should upgrade

As each new version of Illustrator is released, I'm always asked whether upgrading is worthwhile. My answer is always an enthusiastic "Yes!" Besides the benefits of technical support, new versions contain new functions and time-saving features, such as support for more file formats, new plug-in tools and filters, and last-minute fixes to recently discovered problems. For the latest upgrade, call Adobe at **800-833-6687**. (For try-outs of some great third-party plug-ins, check out the *Wow!* disk.)

More compatibility questions?

If, after reading "Computer & System Requirements" (right), you still can't figure out whether your Mac is completely compatible with Adobe Illustrator, try reading the "Specifications" page in your *Apple Macintosh Owner's Guide.* If this still leaves you in the dark, call your local Apple dealer, or the dealer who sold you your computer. If you still need help, you can call Apple's information line— but be prepared to sit on hold. The Apple number is: 1-800-767-2775 (1-800-SOS-APPLE)

This chapter is packed with tips and techniques chosen to help you to use Adobe Illustrator with optimal ease and efficiency. Whether you're a veteran of Illustrator or a relative newcomer, you're likely to find information here that will greatly increase your productivity in Illustrator and help you get up to speed on the latest features. But remember, this chapter is an addendum to, not a replacement for, Adobe Illustrator's *User Guide* or *Tutorial.*

COMPUTER & SYSTEM REQUIREMENTS

Creating artwork on the computer is wonderful and exciting. Blissfully, our computer art tools, including Adobe Illustrator, have seen great improvements in the past few years. Unfortunately, one of the sad facts about us artists demanding and getting better and more powerful software is that the more powerful upgrades might not run on our older computers.

As wonderful as Illustrator is (and it is), and as much as I encourage you to purchase or upgrade to the latest version (and I do), it will not run effectively on older computers such as the Mac Plus, Mac SE/SE 30 or Mac Classic. In order to access all of Illustrator 6's powerful functions, you'll need to have a Macintosh II computer (or newer) with at least 6 MB of RAM.

Very minimum requirements for using Illustrator 6: Macintosh with a 68020 processor (Mac II), 4 MB of RAM *available to Illustrator* (RAM is the memory for the brain of the computer—see Tip "Setting Illustrator RAM," opposite) and System 7 or later, or a Power Macintosh with 5 MB of *available* RAM.

Highly recommended: **8 MB of RAM.** Actually, I consider this the true minimum; you won't be able to do much with less. I suggest you install as much RAM as you can afford. More RAM in your computer means you will be able to run more applications simultaneously, work with more complex documents, and in turn, work more efficiently.

Highly recommended:

A CD-ROM drive (to access the Adobe Illustrator CD). A full installation of Illustrator will take up quite a bit of hard disk space (over 20 MB), but with a CD-ROM, you can "customize" your installation by choosing to install only the Illustrator program, minimal fonts and system files, and the tutorial lessons you'll need (around 8 MB). You can wait to copy the extra fonts, clip art and expert tips as you need them. Feel free to throw out any sample or tutorial files, as you can reinstall them from the CD. A CD-ROM will let you access the *Wow!* CD disk too!

Highly recommended:

Floating point unit (FPU), or "math coprocessor."
Many functions in Illustrator, especially the plug-ins, can utilize a computer's FPU to speed up operations considerably. While all Power Macintosh computers have an FPU built into the processor chip, earlier Macs offered them only as an option. If you don't have an FPU, find out about getting one installed—they're not expensive.

Highly recommended:

Macintosh System 7. As of Illustrator version 6, you'll need to use System 7 or later, so if you're still using System 6, it's time for you to make the leap to the more robust and easier-to-use System 7. Additionally, you'll be able to take advantage of cool, new technologies from Apple such as QuickTime and Drag and Drop, as well as improved features such as an integrated multi-finder and a hierarchical finder. If you feel you'd rather go for a root canal than face the task of upgrading your system software, you might consider hiring an expert to install System 7 for you. Computers are expensive, your time is valuable, and it is a false economy to tackle projects out of your area of expertise—or realm of patience. ☾

In System 7 (or 6 with Multifinder), you must specify how much RAM (memory) is "allocated" to Illustrator. From the desktop, when Illustrator is not open, select the Illustrator icon (single click) and type ⌘-I (File: Get Info). To determine what to set as your

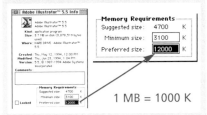

1 MB = 1000 K

"Preferred size," get a pencil and paper. First find out how much RAM you have (choose "About This Macintosh" from the Apple menu). Subtract the MB used for the System, and (if possible) leave a couple MB free for copying, pasting and printing. (With the minimum 5 MB of RAM total, you must set Illustrator to 3100K.) Then with the remaining available RAM, consider how complex the images are that you'll be working with in Illustrator (the more complex, the more RAM you'll need: usually between 5 MB and 25 MB). Finally, how many other programs will you need to be running, and how much RAM do they require?

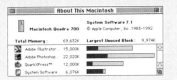

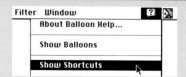
Illustrator 6 includes an online list of keyboard shortcuts and modifier keys: Choose Show Shortcuts (from the Help menu). Always keep your *Adobe Illustrator Quick Reference Card* handy for quick access. Use the indexes and the "Troubleshooting" appendix in the *User Guide* before you panic over a problem. And don't forget to explore thoroughly the *Adobe Illustrator Deluxe CD-ROM* for a wealth of expert advice.

Illustrator on your screen

Illustrator images are drawn on your computer screen using Apple's QuickDraw display language. Depending upon your monitor, QuickDraw, usually displays images in 72 pixels per inch (ppi), which results in seemingly "jaggy" screen images. But don't worry; when you print your image to a PostScript printer, you can do so at the maximum resolution of that printer (this resolution is called "device-dependent resolution"). To copy a 72 ppi PICT QuickDraw version of your selection to the Mac Clipboard (for pasting into a non-Adobe program), choose Option-⌘-C.

WORKING WITH POSTSCRIPT OBJECTS
Anchor points, lines and Bézier* curves

Adobe uses its own language, called "PostScript," to describe mathematically each of the objects that you create in Illustrator. Instead of using pixels to draw shapes, Illustrator creates objects made up of points, called "anchor points." They are connected by outlines (which can be curved or straight) called "paths," and are visible if you work in Artwork viewing mode (⌘-E, or View: Artwork). The PostScript language describes information about the location and size of each path, as well as each path's dozen or so attributes, such as its fill color and outline weight and color. Because you are creating objects, you'll be able to change the order in which the objects stack upon each other. You'll also be able to group objects together so they can be selected as if they were one object, and even ungroup them later, if you wish.

Although you can now work in Illustrator while previewing the path in full color, in many cases you'll find that editing your image in Artwork mode (in which you are viewing the paths in black outline) provides greater accuracy and greatly speeds up the time it takes for Illustrator to redraw the computer screen.

If you took geometry, you probably remember that the shortest distance between two points is a straight line. In Illustrator, this rule translates into each line being defined by two anchor points which are created by clicking with the Pen tool.

In mathematically describing rectangles and circles, Illustrator computes the center, length of the sides or radius, based on the total width and height you specify. For more complex shapes involving freeform curves, Adobe Illustrator allows you to use the Pen tool to create Bézier curves defined by four points: the two anchor points, and two additional points called "direction points." (Although they do not print, they are needed to define the angle and the depth of the curve.) To make these direction points easier to see and manipulate, Illustrator connects each direction point to its anchor point

* Named after the software engineer who pioneered its use, Pierre Bézier

with a nonprinting direction line, also called a "handle." The direction points and handles are visible when you're creating a path with the Pen tool or are editing the path with the Direct-selection tool. While this might all sound complicated to you, and involve some initial awkwardness, manipulating Bézier curves can prove quite intuitive.

More about Bézier curves

If you're new to Bézier curves, you should go through the Adobe *Tutorial* lessons. For some Bézier fine-tuning, I have included some practice lessons on the *Wow!* disk.

If they don't already, your other Mac graphics programs will most likely eventually include Béziers, so you might as well take the time now to get over your discomfort with the Pen tool. Friskets in Painter, paths in Photoshop, and the outline and extrusion curves of many 3D programs all have at their base a Bézier curve, and in many cases, an Adobe PostScript–defined Bézier curve.

The key to learning Béziers is to take your initial lessons in short doses and stop when you get frustrated. Designer Kathleen Tinkel describes Bézier direction lines as "following the gesture of the curve"; this artistic view should help you to create fluid Bézier curves.

And finally, some rules about Bézier curves:

- The length and angle of the handles "anticipate" the curves which will follow.

- The length of handles are equal to approximately $\frac{1}{3}$ the length of the curve, if it were straightened.

- Place anchor points on either side of a bump, and not in between.

- The fewer the anchor points, the smoother the curve will look, and the faster the curve will print.

- Adjust a curve's height and angle by dragging the direction points, or grab the curve itself to adjust its height.

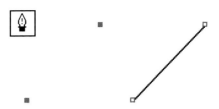

Clicking with the Pen tool to create anchor points for straight lines

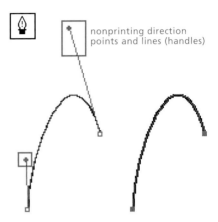

nonprinting direction points and lines (handles)

Click-dragging with the Pen tool to create anchor points and pulling out direction lines for curves

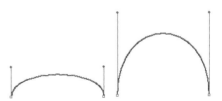

When direction handles are short, curves are shallow; when handles are long, curves are deep

The length and angle of the handles determine the gesture of the curves

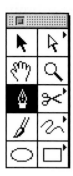

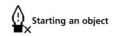
Starting an object

Adding a point

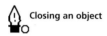
Closing an object

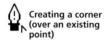
Creating a corner (over an existing point)

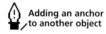
Adding an anchor to another object

Basic cursor objects options for the Pen tool

Correcting common mistakes

Avoid these common mistakes:

- If you try to deselect by clicking outside of your object while you still have the Pen tool, you'll scatter extra points throughout your image, which can cause problems later. If you're aware that you *did* click by mistake, choose Undo (⌘-Z). To check for and remove extra points, choose Artwork mode, look for "x"s (other than in the centers of ovals or rectangles) and choose Filter: Select Stray Points, then delete the selected points.

- If you try to delete an object that had been selected by the Direct-selection tool, only the selected point or path will be deleted. Since what remains of the object will now be fully selected, delete again to remove the entire object.

WATCH YOUR CURSOR!

Illustrator provides cursors that change to indicate not only what tool you have selected, but also which function you are about to perform. If you learn to watch your cursor, you will avoid the most common Illustrator mistakes.

If you choose the Pen tool:

- **Before you start,** your cursor displays as the Pen tool with a "×" This indicates that you're starting a new object.

- **Once you've begun your object,** your cursor changes to a regular Pen. This indicates that you're about to add to an existing object.

- **If your cursor gets close to an existing anchor point,** it will change to a Pen with a "∧" to indicate that you're about to click on top of the last anchor point. If you click-drag on top of the anchor point, you will be re-drawing the curve. If you hold down the Option key while you click-drag on top of the point, then you will pull out a new direction line, creating a corner (like the petals of a flower). If you click (or Option-click) on top of the point, you will collapse the outgoing direction line, allowing you to attach a straight line to the curve.

- **If your cursor gets close to an end anchor point of an object,** it will change to a Pen with a "o" to indicate that you're about to "close" the path. If you do close the path, then your cursor will change back to a Pen with a "×" to indicate that you're beginning a new object.

- **If you use Direct-selection to adjust the object as you go,** then make sure that you look at your cursor when you're ready to continue your object. If it's still a regular Pen, then continue to place the next point, adding to your object. If, instead, the Pen tool has a "×" (indicating that you are about to start a new object), then you must redraw your last point. As you approach the last anchor point, your cursor will change to a Pen with a "/".

Click and drag over this last point to redraw the last curve. To form a corner on the point as you draw, hold down your Option key to click-drag out a new direction line. **Note:** *See Sandee Cohen's "Cursor Clues" chart in the Goodies folder on the* Wow! *disk for more on cursors.*

Bézier-editing tools

Next to the Pen tool in the Toolbox, as a pop-up from the Scissors tool, is a group of tools you can use to edit Illustrator paths. Click and hold on the Scissors tool, and drag to select one of the others. (To learn about *filters* that edit, see *Chapter 6.*)

- **The Scissors tool** cuts a path where you click by adding two disconnected, selected anchor points exactly on top of each other. To select just one of the points, deselect the object, then click with the Direct-selection tool on the spot where you cut to select the upper anchor point and drag it to the side to see the two points better. If your path was open when you cut it with the Scissors tool, then the paths will be split in two so you can see each path, on either side of the cut, separate from the other.

- **The Add-anchor-point tool** adds an anchor point to a path at the location where you click.

- **The Delete-anchor-point tool** deletes an anchor point when you click *directly* on the point.

- **The Convert-direction-point tool** lets you convert an anchor point in an already drawn path from a smooth curve to a corner, from a corner to a smooth curve, or from a smooth curve to a hinged curve (two curves hinged at a point). To convert a curve to a corner, click on the anchor point. To convert a corner to a smooth curve, click-drag on the anchor point counterclockwise to pull out a new direction line (or twirl the point until it straightens out the curve). To hinge a smooth curve, grab the direction point itself and drag it to the new position.

To change your object...

To make changes to a path, first click on it with the Direct-selection tool which displays all anchor points and the direction handles on either side of a selected curve. You can adjust the length and angle of a curve by grabbing and dragging anchor points, direction handles, or the curve itself. If you select an object but don't see any direction handles, you can:

- Deselect it, then try again.
- If you're in Preview mode, be sure to click on the *path itself* or switch to Artwork mode. Or, deselect the Area Select option in General Preferences.

Note: *Only* curves *have handles!*

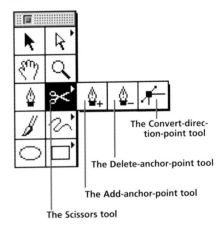

The Convert-direction-point tool

The Delete-anchor-point tool

The Add-anchor-point tool

The Scissors tool

The hollow "snap-to" arrow

As long as "Snap to ☒ Snap to point point" is enabled in General Preferences, you can grab objects from any path or point and drag until they *snap* to a guide or other object; the arrow will turn hollow.

 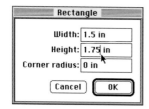

Making a rectangle numerically by choosing the Rectangle tool and clicking in your image to place the upper left-hand anchor point, then numerically entering the other specs

Making a rectangle by choosing the Rectangle tool and clicking and dragging from one corner to the opposite corner

Geometric objects

The Oval and Rectangle tools create objects called "geometric primitives." These geometric objects are mathematically accurate and symmetrical paths that are grouped with a nonprinting anchor point, which indicates the center. Use the centers of the geometric objects to "snap-align" them with each other, or with other objects and guides. You can create these geometric objects numerically or manually (see *Chapter 2* for exercises in creating and manipulating geometric objects). For information on the Polygon, Spiral and Star tools in the Plug-in Toolbox, see *Chapter 6*, page 126.

• **To create a geometric object with numeric input,** select the desired geometric tool, move your cursor into the image window and click to establish the upper left corner of your object. Enter the desired dimensions in the dialog box, and click OK (or hit Return). To create the object numerically from the object's center instead, Option-click in your image window. Or, double-click on the tool first, switching the tool mode to show a "+" in the center, which indicates that the object will be drawn from its center. Holding down the Option key in this case will draw the object from the corner.

• **To create an oval or rectangle manually,** select the desired geometric tool, and click-drag to form the object from one corner to the other. To create the object from the center, hold down the Option key and drag from the center outward (keep the Option key down until you release the mouse button to ensure the "draw from center"). Alternately, double-click on the tool first to switch the tool mode so that a "+" shows in the center, indicating that the object will be drawn from its center. Holding down the Option key in this case will draw the object from the corner. Holding down the Rectangle tool allows you to switch to the Rounded Rectangle tool. Once you have drawn the geometric objects, you can edit them exactly as your other hand-drawn paths. ⌒

GROUPING & SELECTING OBJECTS

To group, or not to group…

Many object-oriented programs (that is, programs that create objects, such as Illustrator and MacDraw) provide you with a grouping function so you can act upon multiple objects as if they were one object. In Illustrator, though, you don't have to group objects or parts of objects to act on them as a unit; you merely have to select them. But, since grouping objects together places all the objects on the same layer, you don't want to group objects unless you actually need to (for more info on layers and reordering objects, see *Chapter 4*).

So when do you want to group objects? Group objects when you need to act on them *repeatedly* as a unit. Take an illustration of a bicycle as an example. Use the Group function (⌘-G, or Edit: Arrange) to group the spokes of a wheel, then group the two wheels of a bicycle, then group the wheels with the frame (⌘-U ungroups). We'll continue referring to this bicycle below:

Selecting within groups

- **With the Direct-selection tool.** Click on a point or path with the Direct-selection tool to select that point or portion of the path. If you click on a spoke of a wheel, you'll select the portion of the spoke's path you clicked upon.

- **With the Selection tool.** Click on an object with the Selection tool to select the largest group containing that object. In our example, it would be the entire bicycle.

- **With the Group-selection tool.** Use the Group-selection tool to select subgroupings. First, click with the Group-selection tool to select the entire spoke path. The second click will result in the entire wheel, the third will be the two wheels, and the fourth will be the entire bicycle.
Note: *Once you've selected objects with the Group-selection tool, if you want to grab and move them, you must change to one of the other selection tools. If you click again with Group-selection tool, you'll be selecting the next group up!*

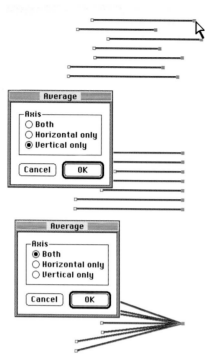

Averaging

Two of Illustrator's most useful functions are Average (⌘-L, or Arrange: Average) and Join (⌘-J, or Arrange: Join). In essence, averaging allows you to align selected *points*. (To align *objects*, choose Filter: Objects: Align.) Use the Direct-selection tool to marquee-select or Shift-select any number of points belonging to any number of objects. Then choose Average to align the selected points horizontally, vertically, or along both axes.

Joining

Whereas the Average command can be performed on any number of points, you can only perform Join on two open endpoints. The Join function will operate differently depending on the objects:

- **If the two open endpoints are exactly on top of each other,** then Join will open a dialog box asking if the join should be smooth (a curved Bézier anchor with direction handles) or a corner (an anchor point with no handles). Both points will fuse into one point.

- **If the two open endpoints are *not* exactly on top of each other,** then Join will create a straight line joining the two points. If you attempt to join two points to fuse as one but you don't get the dialog box, then you have merely added an adjoining straight line! Undo (⌘-Z) and see "Averaging & Joining" below.

- **If you select an open path** (in this case, you don't need to select the endpoints), then Join will close the path.

- **If the two open endpoints are on different objects,** then Join will connect the two paths into one.

Using the Average command to align selected endpoints vertically, then choosing "Both"

Averaging & Joining in one step

Type Option-⌘-J (or -L). The join forms a corner if joining to a line, or a hinged curve if joining to a curve. ☾

Joining warning

If you get an error message that you can't join points, do the following—in addition to the conditions in the warning:

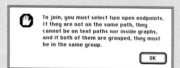

- Make sure that you've selected only *two* points (no third stray point selected by mistake?).
- Make sure that you've selected *endpoints*, not midpoints.

GRAPHING & CHARTING

Through the Graph tool, Illustrator allows you to create charts and graphs in six different styles. The interface isn't designed for those who are new to charts or graphs, so if you intend to use this tool, I suggest you thoroughly read the graph chapter in the *User Guide* and then experiment with the various Graphs & Graph Designs provided by Adobe in the Samples folder. Also, please keep in mind that the purpose of a chart or graph is clear communication of numeric information as a visual aid. No matter how beautiful or slick an illustration is, if it doesn't present your information clearly, it's bad design.

Before you begin, set a default chart or graph style by double-clicking on the Graph tool and choosing the style you want. To actually produce your graph, use the Graph tool very much like the Rectangle tool: either click-drag to create a rectangular object from corner to corner, or hold down the Option key and click with the tool to specify numerically the dimensions of your graph.

After you establish the dimensions, the Graph dialog box will open, awaiting your input of numeric data. Enter labels and numbers by highlighting the desired cell and typing into the entry line along the top. Tab to enter text in the next horizontal cell. You must look carefully in the *User Guide* to determine how you should enter data for the specific graph style you want.

Note: *Unfortunately, it's a bit too simple to enter text accidentally into the wrong field, so be meticulous. Just about the only correction strategy available while you are entering data is to transpose horizontal and vertical data by clicking the Transpose button.*

You can also import data saved in "Tab-delineated" text format. Any word processing, spreadsheet or charting program should let you save or export numbers and labels into text that has been separated by Tabs (to indicate that text elements are related) and Returns (to indicate a new set of related text elements).

To change the style of an existing graph, select the entire graph with the Selection tool and double-click on

Maintaining "graphness"

If you want to continue to work with your graph numerically, *don't*, under any circumstances, ungroup your graph; it will make numerical data changes impossible. To avoid losing the special graph formatting, follow these special precautions:

- Use the Selection tool to select the entire graph for changes in style. Once your graph is selected, 1) Double-click the Graph tool to change the graph style; 2) Choose Object: Graphs: Data to change numeric data; or 3) To apply shaped design elements, see "Customizing graph designs" in this section.
- Use the Group-selection tool to select a category of data, then restyle or recolor as desired.
- Use the Type tool or Direct-selection tool to select and change individual text elements.
- Use the Direct-selection tool to select individual elements to change their styling.

When you *do* ungroup

Once you're *completely* finished numerically adjusting a graph, you may wish to delete some objects. Select the graph (with the Selection tool) and use Ungroup (⌘-U). No longer part of a graph, the objects can now be deleted.

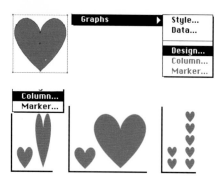

Defining a design; using the heart to create columns vertically scaled; uniformly scaled; forming a repeating design

Using graphs as templates

Many designers use the Graph tool to plot points and generate the scale and legend. They can create an illustration that uses the placement of the graph as a guide (see *Chapter 4* for help in locking the graph for use as a template).

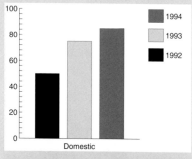

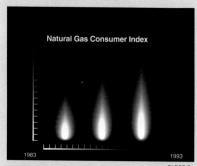

Eve Elberg used the bar graph above as a template to plot the basic points in this illustration. For the glowing effect, she used blends and gradients (see **Chapter 5**).

the Graph tool in the Toolbox. Choose another style and click OK. But be aware that, because different chart and graph styles require different types of data, all charts won't necessarily translate into others.

To reaccess a graph's numeric data, use the Selection tool to select your graph and choose Object: Graphs: Data. But before you try to alter your numeric data, make sure you have saved your graph (there is no Cancel command in the data entry, though you can, of course, use Undo, ⌘-Z).

Customizing graph designs

Being able to insert design elements into a graph is a snazzy—but much overused—aspect of the graphing feature. Illustrator allows you to define graph designs, which can be used as substitutes for rectangular column bars and line markers. For instance, using the "scaling" option, you can take a heart-shaped design and incorporate it into a graph by stretching (vertically scaling) or enlarging (uniformly scaling) the heart to the correct height. A variant of this technique allows you to define a portion of the heart to be scaled (called the "Sliding" Design). By using the "repeating" option, you can get the hearts to stack on top of each other until they reach the correct height.

Defining a graph design element works much the same way as defining a pattern design (see *Chapter 3*). After creating the object(s) you wish to use as a design element, place a rectangle to enclose your design (with no fill or stroke) behind that element (choose Arrange: Send To Back, ⌘-B), select the rectangle with its design and choose Object: Graphs: Design. In the dialog box, click New and name your design. To apply the design, use the Selection tool to select the graph, choose Object: Graphs: Columns and select the desired method of fitting your design to the column size. You can also use design elements to serve as "markers" (indicating plotted points) for line and scatter graph styles. Follow the above procedure but choose Object: Graphs: Marker.

In speaking with the art departments at some of the nation's busiest newspapers and periodicals, I discovered that even though they often finish their charts and graphs in Illustrator, most use other programs to translate numbers into graphics. Included on the *Wow!* disk, however, is the shareware premiere of Chronchart, created by Eric Jungerman for the *San Francisco Chronicle*. Chronchart works with Microsoft's spreadsheet Excel to take any subset of your information (including stipulations such as "the 30 most recent sales over $1000") and transform it into graphs and charts editable by Illustrator. ☺

TRANSFORMATIONS

Moving, scaling, rotating, reflecting and shearing are all operations that transform selected objects or selected portions of objects. Always begin by selecting what you wish to transform. If you're not happy with the transformation you've just applied, use Undo (⌘-Z) before applying a new transformation—or you'll end up applying the new transformation on top of the previous one.

In Illustrator, you can perform all transformations manually (see *Chapter 2* for exercises), or through a dialog box for numeric accuracy for specifying the distance, degree, percentage or angle. From the dialog box, you can also decide whether lines will be scaled, whether to transform a copy of the object and, if appropriate, whether selected objects, patterns that fill the objects, or both, will be transformed. (For more about transforming patterns, see Tip on page 74.)

Illustrator remembers the last transformation you performed, and keeps those numbers in the appropriate dialog box until you transform differently or restart the program. This means that, if the last time you scaled an image numerically, you chose not to scale the line weights, the next time you scale, manually or numerically, your line weights will not be scaled. With Illustrator 6's Control Palette (from the Window menu), you can perform certain transformations numerically with some added features. See ⑥ for more on the Control Palette.

Scaling images to an exact size

There are two ways to scale a selection to an exact size:
- *The new easy way:* Use the fabulous Scale To Dimension filter in the Plug-ins folder on the *Wow!* disk.
- *The old hard way:* Create a "proxy" rectangle the size of your image, then from the upper left corner of the proxy, Option-click to create a rectangle in the target dimensions. Then click with your Scale tool in the upper left, grab the lower right, and drag to scale your proxy to match the target. (Hold Shift if you're scaling to only one dimension.) Delete these rectangles, select your objects, double-click the Scale tool, and apply the settings.

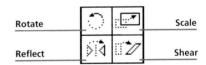

Rotate · Scale

Reflect · Shear

Power transformation

Illustrator remembers the last transformation you performed— from simple moves to rotating a copy of an object. Press ⌘-D (or Arrange: Repeat Transform) to repeat the last transformation.

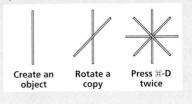

Create an object · Rotate a copy · Press ⌘-D twice

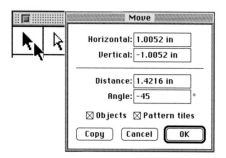

Option-clicking on the Selection tool to access the Move dialog box

Click-dragging the Measure tool to open Info palette, which loads into the Move dialog box

Moving complex images

Create a "proxy" rectangle closely surrounding the objects you wish to move. Move the proxy in one motion to the desired location, then delete it. Select your objects, Option-click the Selection arrow and click OK to apply the proxy's move. Or, numerically relocate using the Control Palette (see ⑥).

If you can't see a new style...

If you're trying to make style changes, but nothing seems to change on the screen, Make sure:
- your objects are selected.
- you are in Preview and not Art-work mode.
- the Auto box in the Paint Style palette is enabled.

Note: *If you disable the Auto box, you'll have to click Apply each time you want to view a style change.*

Moving

In addition to grabbing and dragging objects manually, you can numerically specify a new location: Option-click on the Selection arrow in the Toolbox, or Shift-⌘-M. For help determining the distance you wish to move, select the Measure tool and click-drag the distance you wish to calculate (the Info palette will appear). Then *immediately* open the Move dialog box to see the measured distance loaded automatically and click OK (or hit Return).

Scale, Rotation, Reflection and Shear tools

For scaling, rotation, reflection and shearing of your objects, Illustrator provides four powerful tools. Each of the transformation tools allows you to click (to manually specify the center about which the transformation will occur), then grab your object to transform it. (For practice with manual transformations, see *Chapter 2*.)

To transform your objects numerically, you can specify how the transformation will affect the selected objects:

- **Double-click on a transformation tool** to access the dialog box. This allows you to transform the objects numerically, originating from an object's center.

- **Option-click on your image with the transformation tool** to access the dialog box to transform your objects numerically, originating from where you clicked.

- **Click-drag on your image with a transformation tool** to transform the selected objects, originating from the center of the group of selected objects. ↻

WORKING WITH PALETTES

Illustrator's palettes are accessible via the Window menu. Each palette is unique, but many share common features:

- **You can make most palettes smaller or larger.** If there's a small flag in the lower right corner, click it to shrink/expand the palette. The Paint Style palette (⌘-I) has three sections, which you can view in various combinations, though you can't view the bottom panel alone. In the Paint Style palette, click on the mini-icons representing the part of the palette you wish to see.

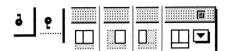

Using the flag, or Paint Style icons, to expand or shrink palettes

- **You must select your object(s) first; then you can make changes to the style.** With your objects selected, you can select any box in the palette containing text (click on the label or in the box) and type. If you're typing something that has limited choices (such as a font or typestyle), then Illustrator will attempt to complete your word; just keep typing until your choice is visible. As you're typing into a text field, use the Tab key to move you around to the other text fields within the palette.

- **IMPORTANT: When you're finished typing into palette text fields, you must hit Return (or Enter).** This action signals to Illustrator that you are ready to enter text somewhere else or resume your illustration.

- **You can edit selective characteristics on multiple objects.** With palettes, you can set one specific style for all selected objects without affecting any other characteristics. For example, your selection might contain multiple objects, one with no stroke, and the rest with outlines of different colors and weights. If, in the Paint Style palette, you set the stroke weight to 1 (point) and leave the other choices unchanged, this action will set the stroke weight of all objects that have strokes to 1 point, but it won't add strokes to unstroked objects, and won't affect the colors of any strokes. You can use this same technique to change assorted text blocks to the same typeface while maintaining differences in type sizes and other formatting.

- **Some palettes have underline toggles that you need to switch between.** In the Paint Style palette, for instance, you click on the appropriate color swatches to switch the underline toggle between Fill and Stroke, or drag color swatches to replace one color with another or

Typing numbers into palettes

To use the current unit of measurement, type the number, and Tab to move to the next text field, or Return. To use another unit of measurement, *follow* the number with "in" or " (inch), "pt" (point), "p" (pica), or "mm" (millimeter), and Return. To resume typing into an *image* text block, press Shift-Return. (*Tip from Sandee Cohen:* Type *calculations* in text fields!)

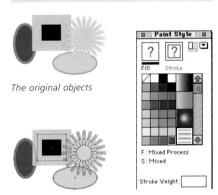

The original objects

Objects selected, and the Paint Style palette indicating that differing styles are selected

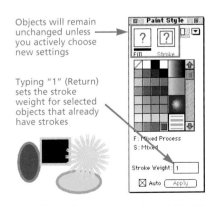

Objects will remain unchanged unless you actively choose new settings

Typing "1" (Return) sets the stroke weight for selected objects that already have strokes

The objects after setting a stroke weight of 1

Black

Save   ⌘S
Save As...
Revert to Saved

to store the swatches in the left side of the palette. You can also click on the square icons to choose one of the color modes: None, White, Black, Process, Custom, Pattern and Gradient. To change a custom color to process color, click on the Process icon. To convert a process color to a custom color, grab the custom color swatch (from Fill, Stroke or the stored colors) and drag it on top of the process swatch. (See *Chapter 3* for more on Paint palettes; see *Chapter 5* for more on Gradient palettes.)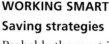

WORKING SMART

Saving strategies

Probably the most important advice I can give you is to save (⌘-S) every few minutes or so. Whenever you make a substantial change to your image, use File: Save As from the File menu and give your image a new name.

Especially since Illustrator files are relatively small in size and save fairly quickly, it's much more time efficient to save incremental versions of your image than it is to reconstruct an earlier version all over again. Back up your work at least once a day before you shut down. Just think to yourself, "If this computer never starts up again, what will I need?" Develop a back-up system using disks, SyQuests, opticals, CDs or DATs (digital audio tapes) so you can archive all of your work. I suggest using a program such as Dantz's Retrospect, which can be set up to search automatically for new and changed files to add to your archives.

I believe in archiving virtually everything and have finally developed a file-naming system that actually helps me keep track of my working process—simplifying my recovery of a working version if necessary. My system involves two components. First, start with a meaningful description of your current image ("hearts compound") and second, add a numerical notation of the version ("1.0"). Keep your numbering system consecutive regardless of the label throughout the entire project. Keep the number in a sequence decimally when you make an incremental change to your image ("1.1, 1.2, 1.3...").

Change to the next numeric sequence when you make a substantive change ("2.0"). In other words, don't start numbers at 1.0 for each phase of the project or you'll be unable to figure out which came first: "Sky 1.0" or "Heart 1.0." If, instead, the labels are "Sky 1.0" and "Heart 4.0," then the creation order is self-explanatory. Finally, make sure that you keep all files in a named and dated folder that distinguishes them from other projects.

For saving in other formats, see "PostScript Printing & Exporting" on page 24.

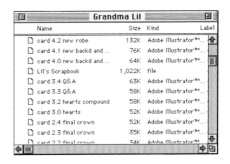

Multiple Undos

Most programs provide you with one chance to undo (⌘-Z) your last move. Illustrator 5 allows you to set the number of Undos (and thus Redos, Shift-⌘-Z), while Illustrator 6 allows you to set the *minimum* number of undos (in General Preferences, for either version).

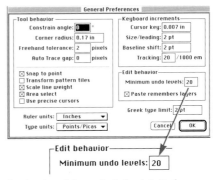

Setting the minimum Undo levels in Preferences

The more RAM (memory) you have available, the more Undo levels you can comfortably set *per document*. I find that setting the level to between 20 and 30 allows me to work freely, and yet keeps me aware that I should still save frequently. Experiment to find the level that works for your system and work style. Be aware that after you set the number of Undos, you must quit and restart the program for a new number of Undos to take effect.

Typing ⌘-Z for Undo (for Redo, type Shift-⌘-Z)

Even after you save a file, your Undos (and Redos) are still available, making it possible to save the current version, undo it to a previous stage and then save it, or continue working from an earlier state. Other actions that are "undo-able" include adding or deleting custom colors, gradients and patterns; grouping or ungrouping; changing the ruler and creating guides. Having 20 to 30 Undos available in each of multiple documents should come close to the experience of having infinite Undos! ↻

How many Undos are left?

The status line in the lower left corner of your image window is actually a pop-up menu that you can toggle between Current Tool, Date and Time, Free Memory, and Number of Undos.

CHANGING YOUR VIEWS
Preview and Artwork

To control the speed of your screen redraw, learn to make use of the various Preview and Artwork modes. Choose

Most of the time you don't have to wait for Illustrator to finish redrawing the Preview before you pull down the next menu or scroll to another location. If you do want to interrupt Illustrator from redrawing your image, type ⌘-. (period). This standard Mac interrupt command will switch from drawing mode to Artwork.

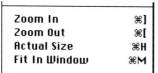

- A speedy way to fit your image to the current window is to double-click on the Hand tool.
- A speedy way to view your image at actual size (100%) is to double-click on the Zoom tool.

Zoom In	⌘]
Zoom Out	⌘[
Actual Size	⌘H
Fit In Window	⌘M

| Window |
| New Window |

With multiple windows open, it's easy to lose track of one window nested behind the others. From the bottom of the Window menu, select the window that you wish to bring to the front.

from the View menu, or type ⌘-E for Artwork, ⌘-Y for Preview or ⌘-Shift-Y for Preview Selection (which leaves everything in Artwork mode except the object(s) currently selected). From the View menu, you can also hide and show templates and guides. (For info on Preview and Artwork modes for individual layers, see *Chapter 4.*)

Zooming in and out

Illustrator provides many ways to zoom in and out:

- **With the Zoom tool.** Click to zoom *in* one level of magnification, hold down the Option key and click to zoom *out* one level. Or, click-drag to define an area, and Illustrator will attempt to fill the current window with the area that you defined.

- **From the View menu.** Choose Zoom In/Out, Actual Size or Fit in Window (see "Zippy zooming" tip at left).

- **By using the shortcut commands for Zoom.** With any tool selected, use ⌘-Spacebar and click to zoom in, Option-⌘-Spacebar and click to zoom out.

New Window

Before Illustrator allowed editing in Preview, New Window was an essential feature. Although Illustrator now allows editing in Preview, New Window is still extremely useful. This allows you to display different views of your current image simultaneously. You can separately zoom each window in or out, resize them, have edges hidden or visible, or set different *layers* to be hidden or locked, in Preview or Artwork (see "Hide Edges/Show Edges" next page, and see *Chapter 4* for more on layers). Most window configurations are saved with the file.

New View

New View allows you to save your current window viewpoint, remembering also your zoom level and which layers are hidden, locked or in Preview mode. Custom views are added to the bottom of the View menu to easily recall a saved view (see *Chapter 4* for more info on views*).*

Hide Edges/Show Edges

If looking at all those anchor points and colored paths distracts you from figuring out what you need to do with selected objects in your current window, choose the Hide Edges toggle from the View menu (or ⌘-Shift-H). Select the toggle again for Show Edges. ⌣

SETTING UP YOUR PAGE

The truth is, controlling your page and printing options is much more difficult than it ought to be. After I explain the different metaphors, please return to the Adobe *User Guide* to get the specific details.

Double-click on the Hand tool to fit your image to your current window. A solid black box representing the size of your Artboard defines the parameters of your final image. A dotted line indicates the margins of the printer which is currently selected.

Page Setup

Change the selected printer and page orientation as you would in any Mac program. Choose File: Page Setup, select your printer from the Paper pop-up menu, and choose portrait or landscape orientation.

Change the Reduce or Enlarge option to scale your image in relation to Page Setup. This is a terrific way to scale something quickly to see how it looks when printed out smaller or larger. A 4" line of a 4-point weight, printed at 25% reduction (the maximum you can reduce), will print as a 1", 1-point line. However, because Page Setup only scales your image in relation to the current printing setup, it will not affect the size of the image when placed into another program or another image. Use View: Hide Page Tiling to hide the dotted lines. Use the Page tool to click and drag the dotted-line page parameters around the Artboard; only the objects within the dotted line will print to your printer.

The Artboard

Think of the Artboard as the final size your image will actually be. To change Artboard size, choose File: Document Setup. To match your current printer, enable Use Page Setup and choose from one of the pop-up presets, or set the size up to 120" by 120" (which switches your paper size to "Custom"). Why might you want your Artboard to be a different size from that of your current printer? Commonly, you might want to create a large image that you will eventually print to an imagesetter, but it first needs to be proofed to your laser printer. If this is the case, choose Page Setup to reduce the image size to fit your current printer. Another option is to "tile" your image onto pages which you can physically paste together to simulate the larger page size. See the *User Guide* for details on the various options for printing tiled pages.

Changing measurement units

Press ⌘-Control-U to cycle through different units of measurement for rulers, Info and Control palettes, and some dialog boxes and filters. Or select units in File: Document Setup (⌘-Shift-D). To set measurement units for all new documents, change the units in General Preferences.

Rulers and Ruler Guides

From the View menu, toggle Illustrator's Show/Hide Rulers (or ⌘-R). The rulers will appear in the unit of measurement you've set in Document Setup.

By default, the origin (where 0,0 is) is in the lower left corner of your image. However, to change the ruler origin, grab the lower right corner (where the vertical and horizontal rulers meet) and drag the crosshair up to the desired location. The zeros of the rulers will then reset to the point where you release your mouse. But beware, resetting your ruler origin will realign all patterns.

To create vertical or horizontal ruler guides, click and drag from one of the rulers into your image. A dotted-line guide will appear where you release your mouse. Guides are automatically locked after you create them, so the easiest way to correct a mistake in placing a new guide is to use Undo (⌘-Z) (this can also reset a moved ruler origin). If you need to alter a guide later, select Object: Guides: Lock, to toggle off the automatic lock. You should note that locking or unlocking guides affects every open document. (For info on using objects to make custom guides, see page 96.) ↻

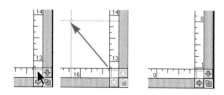

Grabbing and dragging the ruler corner to re-center the ruler origin (zero point)
Note: Resetting the zero point will realign all patterns within objects.

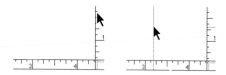

Clicking inside the ruler and dragging into your image to create a vertical or horizontal guide

Quick access to locked guides!

Hold down Shift-Control and click-drag on a guide if you wish to move it. Shift-Control *double-click* to turn it into a selected object that can be deleted. (Tip from *AI Chat News*, see the *Wow!* disk.)

COLOR IN ILLUSTRATOR

Consumer-level monitors, which display color in red, green and blue lights (RGB), cannot yet be made to match four-color CMYK (Cyan, Magenta, Yellow, Black) inks printed onto paper. Therefore, you must retrofit our current technology with partial solutions, starting with calibrating your monitor. The *User Guide* describes a process to achieve some degree of calibration between your program and a specific printer. In addition to this software calibration, methods of hardware calibration are available that actually adjust the beams of the cathode-ray tube emitting the RGB lights. Generally, the larger the monitor, the more inconsistent the color will be in various regions of the screen. Monitor color is also affected by the length of time your monitor is on and the ambient light in your workroom.

Illustrator handles calibration primarily by not letting you mix colors in RGB; you can't even *view* colors that Illustrator deems unprintable. Since you're still viewing in RGB, however, most experts suggest one of two options: The first is to use one of Illustrator's custom color libraries (such as TruMatch and Pantone) in the Color Systems folder. You must then purchase a coordinated swatchbook matching your system so you can choose your colors based on actual four-color printed samples categorized by color families. A different option is to use a four-color printed chart book, like Agfa's *PostScript Color Process Guide*, which provides preprinted samples combining the process colors in 5% increments, organized by the percentages of CMYK inks mixed together. See the *Resource* appendix for contact information on these companies (Agfa, TruMatch and Pantone). ☽

IMAGE INPUT

Illustrator 6 introduces a new concept, that of "image objects": bitmapped images *embedded* in an Illustrator file. Image objects can be created either by rasterizing Illustrator objects (Object: Rasterize), or by placing bitmapped images such as TIFF, PICT, JPEG, etc. (see

CMY Color Model   RGB Color Model

CMY (Cyan, Magenta, Yellow) **subtractive** *colors get darker when mixed; RGB (Red, Green, Blue)* **additive** *colored lights combine to make white*

Trapping issues

Continuous-tone, anti-aliased bitmapped images naturally form "traps" to hide misregistration of CMYK inks, but hard, crisp PostScript edges are a registration nightmare. Some products, such as Island Graphics' IslandTrapper, used for this book, can globally trap pages. If you know the exact size and resolution of your final image, you can rasterize Illustrator files (or specific objects) into bitmaps by using Object: Rasterize, or rasterize in Photoshop (see *Chapter 9*, pages 176–177).

If you don't wish to rasterize:

- Construct your images so that overlapping shapes having common inks form natural traps (see page 64).
- Set individual colors to Overprint in the Paint Style palette.
- Globally set blacks to overprint (Filter: Colors: Overprint Black).
- See the *User Guide* for details on setting traps in *solid* objects using Filter: Pathfinder: Trap.
- For trapping patterns and gradients, see Tip on page 64.

"Other image formats" section below). In contrast to *linked* bitmapped images (see "EPS" section below), image objects can be filtered and permanently altered, but they increase your file size and can slow down your productivity (see Tip "To link or not to link…" at left).

Earlier Illustrator formats

FreeHand, Canvas, and a number of 3D programs allow you to save images in older Illustrator formats. You might also have a document created directly in an earlier version of Illustrator. Instead of double-clicking its icon, drag it onto an Illustrator alias or open an older-format file from within Illustrator by choosing File: Open (⌘-O) and picking the document you want to open. If it's a file you plan to work on or open again, use Save As to save a copy in the current Illustrator format.

EPS (Encapsulated PostScript)

EPS is a "universal" format, meaning that a wide variety of programs support importing and exporting images in EPS format for printing to PostScript printers. In most programs, when saving an image in EPS format, you can choose to include a Preview (the Preview is an on-screen PICT representation of your image; an EPS image placed in another program without a Preview will print properly, but can't be viewed). To import an EPS image into Illustrator, choose File: Place (see *Chapter 4*).

In Illustrator 5.5 all EPS images needed to be Placed and would remain linked to the original file. In Illustrator 6, to link an EPS image, choose the "Placed EPS" option. "Parsed EPS" allows you to directly open any EPS (such as a QuarkXPress EPS page) or PostScript file (such as a file "printed to disk") as editable Illustrator objects (see ⑥ for more details).

Other image formats

Illustrator 6 supports a wealth of file formats (TIFF, PICT, Photoshop, etc.). When opened or placed, most of these are *embedded* into your document, where plug-ins and filters can be applied to them, while other formats remain *linked*. See the latest *User Guide* and Adobe *Read Me* files for up-to-date listings of supported formats (see ⑥ for clarification of linked versus embedded images, and suggested usage). You can also open and edit PDF (Acrobat format) documents directly from within Illustrator.

A number of PICT formats exist, but they can be categorized into two main variations: 1) bitmapped PICTs created in photo-manipulation and painting programs (such as Photoshop and MacPaint) and 2) object PICTs created in drawing programs (such as MacDraw).

Both bitmapped and object PICTs can be opened as Illustrator templates: Choose Open, select the PICT, choose "Illustrator Template (PICT)" and click OK. (For help in optimizing bitmapped PICTs for use as templates, see *Chapter 4*, page 80.)

In contrast to this Template option, the other choice, PICT, allows you to directly open *object* PICTs as editable Illustrator objects, but it is always preferable to save them in Illustrator format if your drawing program provides the PICT option. Bitmapped PICTs, however, are handled differently by this option. Illustrator 5 simply gives you an error message, while Illustrator 6 opens the bitmap as an image object, like any other bitmap format that can be opened by Illustrator 6 (see ⑥).

You should also know that programs such as Canvas and SuperPaint can create combination object/bitmapped PICTs, but, since Illustrator deals with objects and bitmaps differently, be careful to create one *or* the other when you are preparing an image for import to Illustrator.

Importing colors and styles

There are two ways to bring colors and styles into Illustrator. The first, and most efficient, is simply to open a document that includes the styles you want. Styles and colors in any open document are automatically listed and accessible to all other open documents. When you save your image, only the colors or styles that were actually used will be saved with that document—keeping your file

Many ways to copy an object

- Type ⌘-C (Edit: Copy) to copy the object from the Mac Clipboard so it can be pasted into another document or program supporting "PostScript on the Clipboard," such as Adobe's Dimensions or Photoshop.
- Grab the object and hold down the Option key as you transform it or drag it to another location.
- Click the Copy button in any Transformation dialog box (see page 13).
- In the Layers palette, Option-drag the dot representing the selected objects from one layer to another. (See *Chapter 4* for more on layers.)
- Using Illustrator 6 with System 7.5, you can simply "drag and drop" selected objects from one document to another, as well as to other programs supporting "PostScript on the Clipboard."

Change that style name!

IMPORTANT: When Illustrator opens a style that has the same name as a style currently open, it will *replace* the previously current style with the newly opened one. Therefore, when you change the definition of a style, make certain to change its name as well!

First and foremost, use Save As to save incremental versions of your image while you work (see "Saving strategies," page 16, and "Exporting Illustrator to other programs," facing page). From Save As you can also choose to save in a variety of formats. Since you'll lose editing capability (and certain features, such as layers) with other formats, use them if (and only if) you plan to open your image in a program that cannot understand your current version of Illustrator. Save in Acrobat PDF (Portable Document Format) for faxing, sending to clients who don't have Illustrator, or publishing on the Web. For PDF details see the guide provided with the Acrobat Reader installed from the *Adobe Illustrator Deluxe CD-ROM.*

Proofing your prints

Get into the habit of proofing all your images to a laser printer to gauge whether your image will print relatively slowly or faster. The higher the resolution you are printing to, the longer your PostScript image will take to print. Based on your laser test, if you know that your image will require hours to print, then you might be able to arrange with your service bureau to print your image overnight or on a weekend to save you extra charges.

small. When you install Illustrator, Adobe includes many custom styles for your use in the folders for Color Systems, Gradients, and Patterns. Open the file of your choice, size the window small (to take up the minimal amount of RAM) and then bring your image window to the front. As long as the style document is open, you'll have full access to it through the appropriate palettes.

The other way is to choose Import Styles from the File menu. When you import styles (patterns, color systems or gradients), the styles are saved with your document. Although this is convenient, it can make your files very large. You can import styles or colors from any Illustrator document. ○

POSTSCRIPT PRINTING & EXPORTING

When you're ready to print your image (to a laser or inkjet printer, imagesetter or film recorder), you should use a PostScript printing device. Adobe owns and licenses the PostScript language, making PostScript printers somewhat more expensive than QuickDraw or other non-PostScript printers. Some companies produce PostScript-compatible printers or provide PostScript emulation. Illustrator images sometimes print just fine to these printers, but at other times, you might run into problems. Also, it generally takes longer to print to non-PostScript printers, while PostScript Level 2 printers provide better printing clarity, even faster printing, and some special effects. In general, the newer the PostScript device, the faster and less problematic your printing will be. The more memory you install in your printer, the quicker your text and images will print. Finally, for crucial jobs you must develop good relations with your service bureaus, and get in the habit of running test prints to identify possible problems.

Correcting printing problems

When printing Illustrator 5.0 files, many artists (including me) experienced some particularly hideous printing errors and anomalies. Most of those have been corrected

in more recent versions of Illustrator, so if you have a 5.0 image, open it in your current version and resave the image. If you *still* have trouble printing (most likely to an older imagesetter), you have two other options. The first is to choose File: Document Setup, enable "Compatible gradient printing" and resave; this can cause the image to print more slowly to newer imagesetters, so don't use it unless you have to. The fallback solution is to save a copy of the file in Illustrator 3.2 format with the suffix ".Ill3" (to let you know that it is Illustrator 3 format).
IMPORTANT: *Saving in Illustrator 3.2 format converts all your gradients into blends, eliminating the capacity to re-edit the gradients (see* Chapter 5 *for gradients and blends).*

Exporting Illustrator to other programs
Unlike continuous-tone, bitmapped images, which tend to get very large in size, many Adobe Illustrator–format images remain small—and even fit on a floppy disk. However, to place your Illustrator image into a program such as PageMaker or QuarkXPress, you must save a copy of your image in EPS format, which increases the file size.

Bringing your Illustrator image into Adobe Photoshop is a bit easier. When you copy and paste from Illustrator to Photoshop 3.0, you can paste objects styled the way they were in Illustrator, or paste them as nonprinting *paths* to use for selection. You can also "drag and drop" between Illustrator 6 and Photoshop 3.04 in System 7.5. Or you can choose to Place images created in one program into the other. For more on Photoshop/Illustrator compatibility, see Tip at right, *Chapter 9* and ⑥.

More about controlling the size of your files
The major factors that can increase your file size are the inclusion of image objects, Path Pattern and Ink Pen objects, complex patterns, a large number of blends and gradients, and linked bitmapped images. Although linked bitmaps can, in themselves, be large, the same image, embedded as an image object is significantly larger. If your Illustrator file *does* include placed EPS images, and you

Document Setup... ⌘⇧D
☒ Use printer's default screen
☐ Compatible gradient printing
OK
Use this option only when you're having trouble printing gradients to level 1 printers. See the documentation for more information.
OK

For correcting problems in printing, try the "Compatible gradient printing" option

If Photoshop won't open it...
Although this might change in later versions of Photoshop, Photoshop 3 can't import some Illustrator elements such as patterns and linked image files. In Illustrator 6 you can circumvent this problem by converting patterns to objects (choose Object: Expand) and replacing EPS files with TIFF image objects. Use the Control palette both to note the coordinates of your EPS and to relocate your new image object. (For more on the symbiotic relationship between these two programs, see *Chapter 9*, ⑥, and the User Guides for Illustrator and Photoshop.)

Placing bitmaps in Illustrator
In Illustrator, placed EPS bitmapped images are linked to the original file (keeping the Illustrator file itself relatively small). Other bitmapped formats placed into Illustrator might actually become embedded into your document, increasing your file size *dramatically*. See ⑥ for details.

Saving time and space

Note: *Before you attempt to minimize the size of your file, make certain that you're working on a copy. And, make sure that you don't have any other files open—especially "style sheet" documents—because you'll end up deleting the unused styles in all open documents!*

To minimize the size of your file, first remove all your unused colors and patterns. Open the appropriate palette, click "Select all unused," then delete (this action *usually* can be undone). You should also minimize the time it takes to print an Illustrator file, even if it's been placed into another program, such as QuarkXPress or PageMaker (for details on saving for export, see the entire section starting on page 24 "PostScript Printing & Exporting"). If you've scaled or rotated an Illustrator image once it's been placed into another program, note the numeric percentages of scaling and the degrees of rotation. Next, reopen the file in Illustrator, perform the identical scale or rotation, then re-place this pre-transformed version into the other program, making sure to reset the scaling and rotation for this already transformed image to zero. IMPORTANT: *Be certain to scale line weight, objects and pattern tiles when you perform these transformations in Illustrator (see page 13).*

need to save the entire file in EPS format (for placement into, and printing from, other programs), you'll have the option to "Include Placed Images." I highly recommend this option, as it will embed placed images into your Illustrator file and make printing from page layout programs and film recorders much more predictable. However, since including placed images will further increase the file size, wait until you've completed an image and are ready to place it into another program before you save a copy with placed images embedded. Whether or not you choose to embed placed images, you *must* collect all of the files which have been placed into your Illustrator documents and transport them along with your Illustrator file. So, although the EPS format is essential for bringing images into Illustrator, and Illustrator images into other programs, be mindful that EPS files will inevitably add bulk to the transportation of your image.

Printing speed

A related, but even more crucial factor to take into consideration when creating an image is understanding what elements make an image take longer to print. Special effects, such as transforming or masking placed images, or using complex patterns, or a slew of patterns or a gradient, are the worst culprits for increasing file size and, thus, printing time.

If you perform all scaling and transforming of your EPS images before placing them into Illustrator, you'll greatly reduce your printing time, and if you're scaling down bitmaps, you'll substantially reduce the size of your placed file. Another reason to scale your bitmapped images before placing them in Illustrator is to ensure that the pixel-per-inch resolution of the images is 1.5 to 2 times the size of the line screen at which the final image will be printed. For instance, if your illustration will be printed at 2" by 2" in a 150-line screen, then the resolution of your bitmapped image should not exceed 300 pixels per inch at 2" by 2". Talk to your service bureau and print shop before you make these decisions. ◡

The Zen of Illustrator

2

The Zen of Illustrator

Zen: *"Seeking enlightenment through introspection and intuition rather than scripture."**

You're comfortable with the basic operations of your computer. You've conquered the Adobe Illustrator *Tutorial*. You've committed enough hours to Illustrator to be familiar with how each tool in the palette (theoretically) functions. You even understand how to make Bézier curves. Now what? How do you take all this knowledge and turn it into a mastery of the medium?

As with learning any new artistic medium (such as engraving, watercolor or airbrush), learning to manipulate the tools is just the beginning. Thinking and seeing in that medium is what really makes those tools part of your creative arsenal. Before you can determine the best way to construct an image, you have to be able to envision at least some of the possibilities. The first key to mastering Illustrator is to understand that Illustrator's greatest strength comes not from its myriad tools and functions but from its extreme flexibility in terms of how you construct images. The first part of this chapter, therefore, introduces you to a variety of approaches and techniques for creating and transforming objects.

Once you've got yourself "thinking in Illustrator," you can begin to *visualize* how to achieve the final results. What is the simplest and most elegant way to construct an image? Which tools will you use? Then, once you've begun, allow yourself the flexibility to change course and try something else. Be willing to say to yourself: How else can I get the results that I want?

The second key to mastering Illustrator (or any new medium) is perfecting your hand/eye coordination. In Illustrator, this translates into being proficient enough with the "power-keys" to gain instant access to the tools and functions through the keyboard. With both eyes on the monitor, one hand on the mouse, and the other hand on the keyboard, an experienced Illustrator user can create and manipulate objects in a fraction of the time required otherwise. The second part of this chapter helps you to learn the "finger dance" necessary to become a truly adept power-user.

The ability to harness the full power of Illustrator's basic tools and functions will ultimately make you a true master of Adobe Illustrator. Treat this chapter like meditation. Take it in small doses if necessary. Be mindful that the purpose of these exercises is to open up your mind to possibilities, not to force memorization. When you can conceptualize a number of different ways to create an image, then the hundreds of hints, tips, tricks, and techniques found elsewhere in this book can serve as a jumping-off point for further exploration. If you take the time to explore and absorb this chapter, you should begin to experience what I call the "Zen of Illustrator." This magical program, at first cryptic and counter-intuitive, can help you achieve creative results not possible in any other medium.

※ Adapted from *Webster's New World Dictionary of the English Language*

Building Houses

Sequential Object Construction Exercises

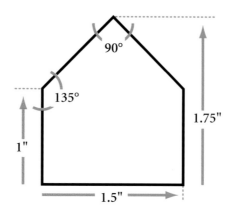

Overview: *Explore different approaches to constructing the same object with Illustrator's basic construction tools.*

This sequence of exercises explores different ways to construct the same simple object, a house. The purpose of these exercises is to introduce you to the flexibility of Illustrator's object construction, so don't worry if some exercises seem less efficient than others. In General Preferences, set Inches for Ruler units (so you can use the numbers provided and the house measurements above). Review *Chapter 1* if you need more help with guides or rectangles. And please read through the recommendations below for preparing your working environment.

1 Work in Artwork mode. Doing so keeps you from being distracted by fills or line weights and lets you see the centers of geometric objects (marked by "×").

2 Use Show Rulers and Show Info. Choose Show Rulers from the View menu (⌘-R) so you can "pull out" guides. Choose Window: Show Info to view numeric data as you work (I arrived at these numbers just this way!), or ignore the numeric data and just draw the houses by eye.

Choosing Window: Show Info (or type ⌘-Control-I) to open Info

3 Read through the *Wow! Glossary*. Please make sure you understand the *Glossary* on the inside back cover.

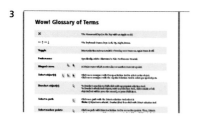

4 Use "modifier" keys. These exercises occasionally use the Shift and Option keys, which you must hold down until *after* you release your mouse button. If you make a mistake, choose Undo (⌘-Z) and do it again.

Hint: *Hold down the Shift key to constrain movement to horizontal/vertical direction. For more modifier key help, see the end of this chapter for the "Finger Dance" lesson.*

Exercise #1:

Use Add-anchor-point tool

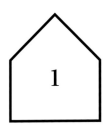

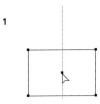

1 Create a rectangle and a vertical guide. Create a wide rectangle (1.5" x 1") and drag out a vertical guide that snaps to the center.

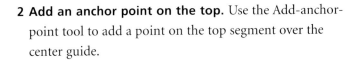

2 Add an anchor point on the top. Use the Add-anchor-point tool to add a point on the top segment over the center guide.

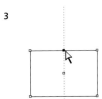 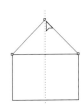

3 Drag the new point up. Use the Direct-selection tool to grab the new point and drag it up into position (.75" for a total height of 1.75").

Exercise #2:

Make an extra point

1 Create a rectangle, delete the top path and place a center point. Create a wide rectangle (1.5" x 1"). With the Direct-selection tool, select the top path and delete it. With the Pen tool, place a point on top of the rectangle center point.

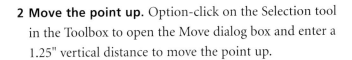

2 Move the point up. Option-click on the Selection tool in the Toolbox to open the Move dialog box and enter a 1.25" vertical distance to move the point up.

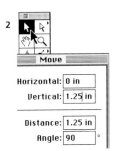 

3 Select and join the point to each side. Use the Direct-selection tool to select the left two points and join (⌘-J) them to the top point. Repeat with the right two points.

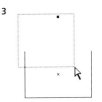 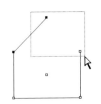

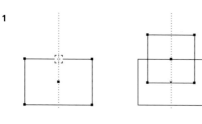

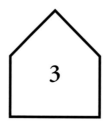

Exercise #3:
Rotate and unite

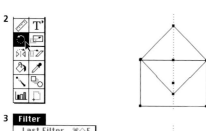

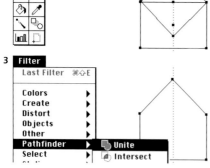

1 Create two rectangles, one centered on the other. Create a wide rectangle (1.5" x 1") and drag out a vertical guide snapping it to the center. With the Option key down, click with the Rectangle tool (Option-click) on the center guide (on the top segment). Enter 1.05" x 1.05".

2 Rotate one rectangle. Double-click the Rotate tool to rotate the new rectangle around its center and enter 45°.

3 Select and unite the rectangles. Marquee-select both shapes and choose Filter: Pathfinder: Unite.

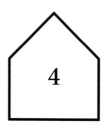

Exercise #4:
Make a six-sided polygon

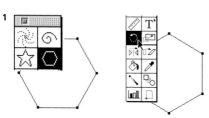

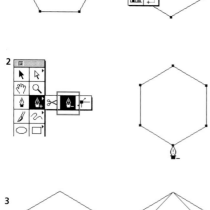

1 Create a six-sided polygon. With the Polygon Plug-in tool selected, Option-click and enter 6 sides and a .866" radius. Then double-click the Rotate tool, and enter 30°.

2 Delete the bottom point. With the Delete-anchor-point tool, click on the bottom point to delete it.

3 Move the two bottom points down, then the two middle points. Use the Direct-selection tool to select the bottom two points. Then grab one of the points and Shift-drag in a vertical line (down .423"). Lastly, Direct-select, grab and Shift-drag the middle two points down vertically into position (down .275").

Exercise #5:

Use Add Anchor Points filter in a three-sided polygon

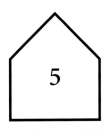

1 Create a three-sided polygon. With the Polygon Plug-in tool selected, Option-click and enter 3 sides, and 1.299" for the Radius.

2 Use the Add Anchor Points filter. With the polygon still selected, choose Filter: Objects: Add Anchor Points.

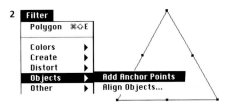

3 Average the left two points, then average the right two points. Direct-select the left two points and average them along the vertical axis (⌘-L, or Object: Average), then repeat for the right two points.

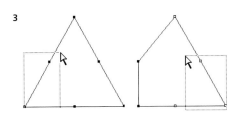

4 Delete the bottom point. With the Delete-anchor-point tool, click on the bottom point to delete it.

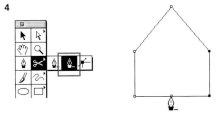

5 Move the top point down. Use the Direct-selection tool to select the top point, then Option-click on the Selection tool itself in the Toolbox to open the Move dialog box and enter a −.186" vertical distance.

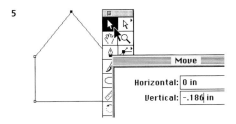

6 Slide in the sides towards the center. Use the Direct-selection tool to click on the right side of the house and drag it towards the center until the roofline looks smooth (hold down your Shift key to constrain the drag horizontally). Repeat for the left side of the house. Alternately, select the right side and use the ← key on your keyboard to nudge the right side towards the center until the roofline looks smooth. Then, select the left side and use the → key to nudge *it* towards the center. (If necessary, change your Cursor-key setting in General Preferences.)

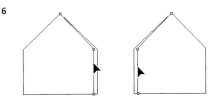

Exercise #6:

Cut a path and
Paste In Front

1 Cut, paste, then move the bottom of a triangle. With the Polygon Plug-in tool selected, Option-click and enter 3 sides, and .866" for the Radius. With the Direct-selection tool, select and cut the bottom path to the Clipboard (⌘-X). Choose Edit: Paste In Front (⌘-F), then grab the bottom path and drag it into position (down .423").

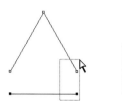

2 Create the sides and move the middle points into place. Use the Direct-selection tool to select the two right points and join them (⌘-J), then repeat for the left two points. Finally, select the two middle points, grab one of them and drag them both into position (up .275").

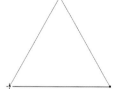

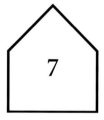

Exercise #7:

Join two objects

1 Make two objects. Option-click with the Polygon tool, enter 3 sides and a .866" Radius. Zoom in on the lower left corner and, with the Rectangle tool, click exactly on the lower left anchor point. Set the rectangle to 1.5" x 1".

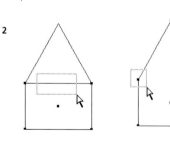

2 Delete the middle and join the corners. Direct-select marquee the middle bisecting lines and delete. Select the upper-left corner points and Option-Join (Option-⌘-J or -L) to average and join simultaneously. Select and Option-Join the upper right points.

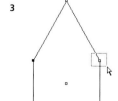

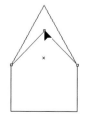

3 Drag the top point down. Grab the top point, hold the Shift key and drag it into position (down .55").

Exercise #8:

Use Add Anchor Points filter, then Option-Join

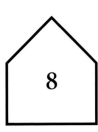

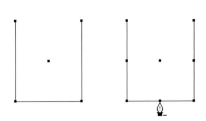

1 **Make a tall rectangle, delete the top path, add anchor points and remove the bottom point.** Create a tall rectangle (1.5" x 1.75") and delete the top path. Then choose Filter: Objects: Add Anchor Points and use the Delete-anchor-point tool to remove the bottom point.

2 **Select and Option-Join the top points and move the middles into position.** Direct-select the top two points and Option-Join them (Option-⌘-J or -L). Then Direct-select the middle points, grab one, and with the Shift key, drag them both up into position (up .125").

Exercise #9:

Reflect a Pen profile

1 **Create a house profile.** Drag out a vertical guide, then reset the ruler origin on the guide. To draw the profile, use the Pen tool to click on the guide at the ruler zero point, and Shift (to constrain your lines to 45° angles) and click to place the corner (.75" down and .75" to the left) and the bottom (1" down).

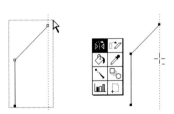

2 **Reflect a copy of the profile.** Select all three points of the house profile, and with the Reflect tool, Option-click on the guide line. Enter an angle of 90° and click Copy.

3 **Join the two profiles.** Direct-select and Join (⌘-J) the bottom two points. Then Direct-select the top two points and Option-Join the peak (Option-⌘-J or -L).

A Classic Icon

Five Ways to Re-create Simple Shapes

Overview: *Finding different ways to construct the same iconic image.*

McSHANE, ADIGARD/M.A.D.

You can construct even the simplest of iconic images in myriad ways. Patricia McShane and Erik Adigard of the M.A.D. graphics firm designed this classic logo for the *Computers Freedom & Privacy* annual conference, which addresses the effects of computer and telecommunications technologies on societal and personal freedom and privacy. This simple iconic representation of an eye is a perfect example of how you can explore different ways to solve the same graphics problem.

1

The Artwork view of the original logo

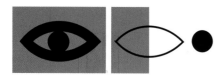

The original logo, constructed from a stroked line and a solid circle

1 First, construct your logo in the way that seems most logical to you. Everybody's mind works differently, and the most obvious solutions to you might seem innovative to the next person. Follow your instincts as to how to construct each image. But if design changes require you to rethink your approach (for instance, what if the client wanted a radial fill instead of the black stroke?), then try something slightly, or even completely, different.

Viewed in Artwork mode, the original *Computers Freedom & Privacy* logo is clean and elegant with a minimum number of anchor points and lines. The M.A.D. team constructed the eye from a stroked line (made with the Pen tool) and a filled, black circle.

2 Make the outer eye shape. Create the solid black, almond-shaped object any way you wish: Try drawing it with the Pen tool like M.A.D. did, or maybe convert an oval into the correct shape by clicking on the middle points with the Convert-direction-point tool.

3 Try using solid objects. Starting with your base object, construct the eye with overlapping solid objects. Scale a version of the outline for the green inset and place a black circle on the top.

4 Try making a compound object. Use the objects that you created in the previous version to make a compound object that allows the inner part of the eye to be cut out. Select the outer black outline and the inner green inset and choose Object: Compound Paths: Make (⌘-8).

5 Try making the eye from a symbol font. Included on the *Wow!* disk is a sample international symbol font from Image Club called "Mini Pics." The character "W" is an eye very close to our icon. Load your Mini Pics font (see your Apple Systems manual for loading fonts), click with the Type tool and type the character "W." Then, choose Object: Create Outlines. This command converts the letter into a compound object different from the one you made in version 4 (above), with three objects cut out of the outline. Since the eye you're trying to make doesn't have a dark solid center, use the Direct-selection tool to select and delete the center compound object. Then try to match the original eye by adjusting the remaining compound paths with the Direct-selection and Scale tools.

Converting and transforming this symbol font may be a convoluted way to create such a simple shape, but the technique is certain to come in handy.

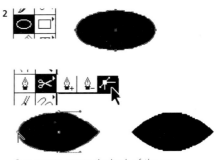

2

One way to create the back of the eye

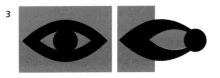

3

Constructing the logo with three solid objects

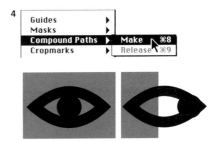

4

Constructing the logo from an outer compound object and an inner solid circle

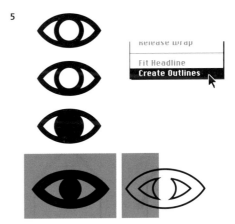

5

The same logo constructed from a text object converted to an outline, then scaled

Zen Scaling

Note: *Use the Shift key to constrain proportions.* ***Zen Scaling*** *practice is also on the* ***Wow!*** *disk.*

1 Scaling proportionally towards the top Click at the top, grab lower-right (LR), drag up

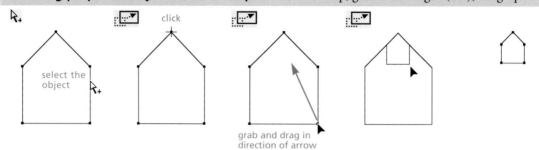

2 Scaling horizontally towards the center Click at the top, grab LR, drag inwards

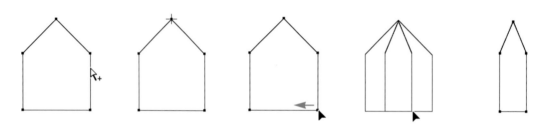

3 Scaling vertically towards the top Click at the top, grab LR, drag straight up

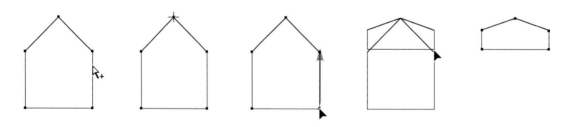

4 Scaling vertically and flipping the object Click at the top, grab LR, drag straight up

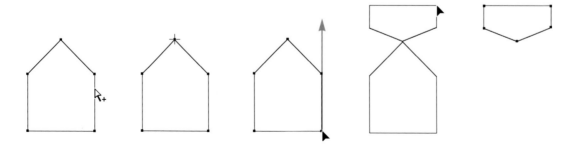

Zen Scaling *(continued)*

Note: *Use the Shift key to constrain proportions.* ***Zen Scaling*** *practice is also on the* ***Wow!*** *disk.*

5 Scaling proportionally towards lower-left (LL) Click LL, grab upper-right, drag to LL

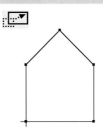 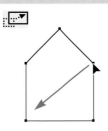 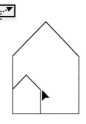

6 Scaling horizontally to the left side Click LL, grab lower-right (LR), drag to left

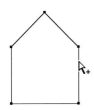  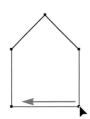  

7 Scaling vertically towards the bottom Click center bottom, grab top, drag down

 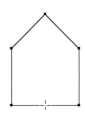 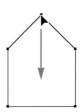 

8 Scaling proportionally towards the center Click the center, grab corner, drag to center

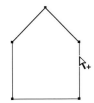 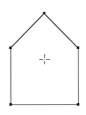  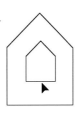

Or, to scale about the center, use the Scale tool to click-drag outside the object towards the center

Zen Rotation ↻

Note: *Use the Shift key to constrain movement.* ***Zen Rotation*** *practice is also on the* ***Wow!*** *disk.*

1 Rotating around the center Click in the center, then grab lower-right (LR) and drag

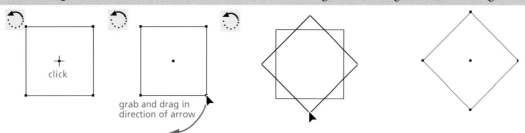

Or, to rotate about the center, use the Rotate tool to click-drag outside the object towards the center

2 Rotating from a corner Click in the upper left corner, then grab LR and drag

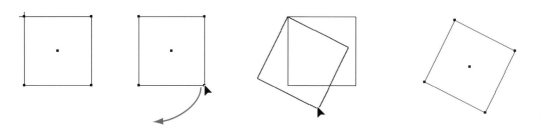

3 Rotating from outside Click above the left corner, then grab LR and drag

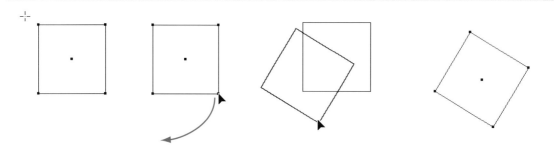

4 Rotating part of a path Marquee points with the Direct-selection tool, then use Rotate tool

Marquee the forearm with Direct-selection tool   *With the Rotate tool, click on the elbow, grab the fingers and drag it around*

Creating a Simple Object Using the Basic Tools

Key: *Click where you see a* RED *cross, grab with the* GRAY *arrow and drag towards* BLACK *arrow.*

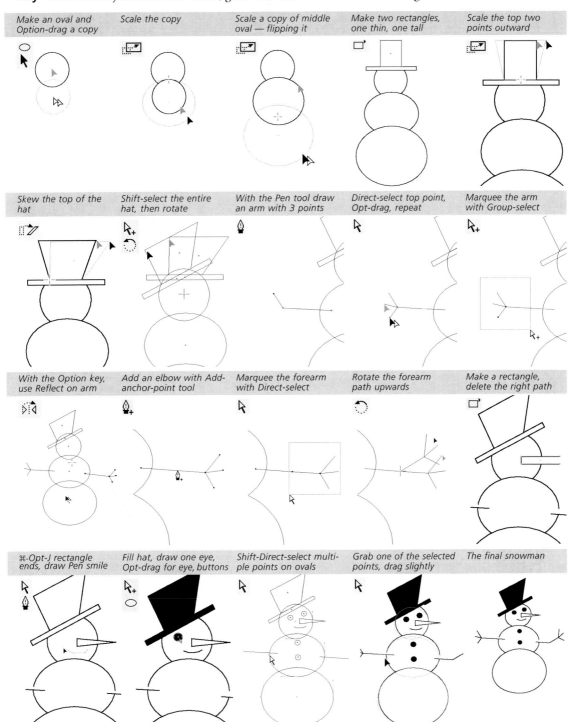

Make an oval and Option-drag a copy

Scale the copy

Scale a copy of middle oval — flipping it

Make two rectangles, one thin, one tall

Scale the top two points outward

Skew the top of the hat

Shift-select the entire hat, then rotate

With the Pen tool draw an arm with 3 points

Direct-select top point, Opt-drag, repeat

Marquee the arm with Group-select

With the Option key, use Reflect on arm

Add an elbow with Add-anchor-point tool

Marquee the forearm with Direct-select

Rotate the forearm path upwards

Make a rectangle, delete the right path

⌘-Opt-J rectangle ends, draw Pen smile

Fill hat, draw one eye, Opt-drag for eye, buttons

Shift-Direct-select multiple points on ovals

Grab one of the selected points, drag slightly

The final snowman

A Finger Dance

Turbo-charge with Illustrator's Power-keys

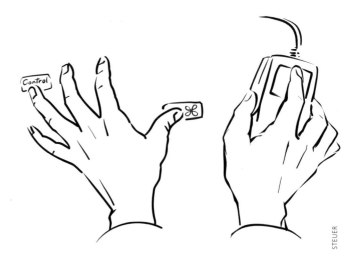

Overview: *Save hours of production time by mastering the finger dance of Illustrator's power-keys.*

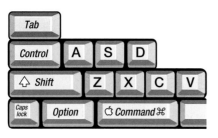

Find a summary of Finger Dance power-keys inside the back cover flap.

1

If you are using the mouse to choose your selection tools from the Toolbox, then you need this lesson. With some time and patience, you'll be able to free up your mouse so that practically the only thing you do with it is draw. Your other hand will learn to dance around the keyboard accessing all of your selection tools, modifying your creation and transformation tools, using your Zoom and Hand tools, and last but not least, providing instant Undo and Redo.

This "Finger Dance" is probably the most difficult aspect of Illustrator to master. Go through these lessons in order, but don't expect to get through them in one or even two sittings. When you make a mistake, use Undo (⌘-Z). Try a couple of exercises, then go back to your own work, incorporating what you've just learned. When you begin to get frustrated, take a break. Later—hours, days, weeks or months later—try another lesson. And don't forget to breathe.

Rule #1: Always keep your thumb on the ⌘ key.
Whether you are using a mouse or a pressure-sensitive tablet, the hand you are not drawing with should be resting on the keyboard, with your thumb on the ⌘ key. This position will make that all-important ⌘-Z (Undo) instantly accessible.

Rule #2: Undo if you make a mistake. This is so crucial an aspect of working in the computer environment that I am willing to be redundant. If there is only one key combination that you memorize, make it ⌘-Z, Undo.

Rule #3: The ⌘ key turns your cursor into a selection tool. In Illustrator, the ⌘ key does a lot more than merely provide you with easy access to Undo (⌘-Z). The ⌘ key will convert any tool into the selection arrow that you last used. In the exercises that follow, you'll soon discover that the most flexible selection arrow is the Direct-selection tool.

Rule #4: Watch your cursor. If you learn to watch your cursor, you'll be able to prevent most errors before they happen. And if you don't (for instance, if you drag a copy of an object by mistake), then use Undo and try again. (See Sandee Cohen's "Cursor Clues" in the Goodies archive on the *Wow!* disk.)

Rule #5: Pay careful attention to *when* you hold down each key. Most of the modifier keys operate differently depending on *when* you hold each key down. If you obey Rule #4 and watch your cursor, then you'll notice what the key you are holding does.

Rule #6: Hold down the key(s) until after you let go of your mouse button. In order for your modifier key to actually modify your action, you *must* keep your key down until *after* you let go of your mouse button.

Rule #7: Work in Artwork mode. When you are constructing or manipulating objects, get into the habit of working in Artwork mode. Of course, if you are designing the colors in your image, you'll need to work in Preview, but as you learn how to use the power-keys, you'll generally find it much quicker and easier if you are in Artwork mode.

2

3

4

Remove "Easy Access"!
When you're using Illustrator, you must take the Apple program called *Easy Access* out of the Extensions folder (in the System folder). Although *Easy Access* was developed as an aid to mouse movements for people with limited manual mobility, it interferes with Illustrator's normal functioning. If you have limited manual dexterity, try using QuickKeys to simplify menu selection, keystrokes and object creation.

7

Note: *Before you begin this sequence of exercises, choose the Direct-selection tool, then select the Rectangle tool and drag to create a rectangle.*

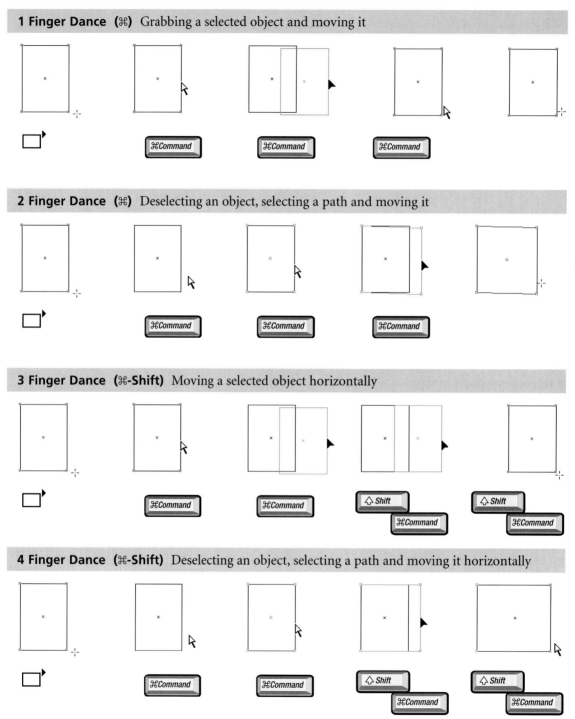

1 Finger Dance (⌘) Grabbing a selected object and moving it

2 Finger Dance (⌘) Deselecting an object, selecting a path and moving it

3 Finger Dance (⌘-Shift) Moving a selected object horizontally

4 Finger Dance (⌘-Shift) Deselecting an object, selecting a path and moving it horizontally

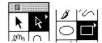

5 Finger Dance (⌘, then ⌘-Option) Moving a copy of a selected object

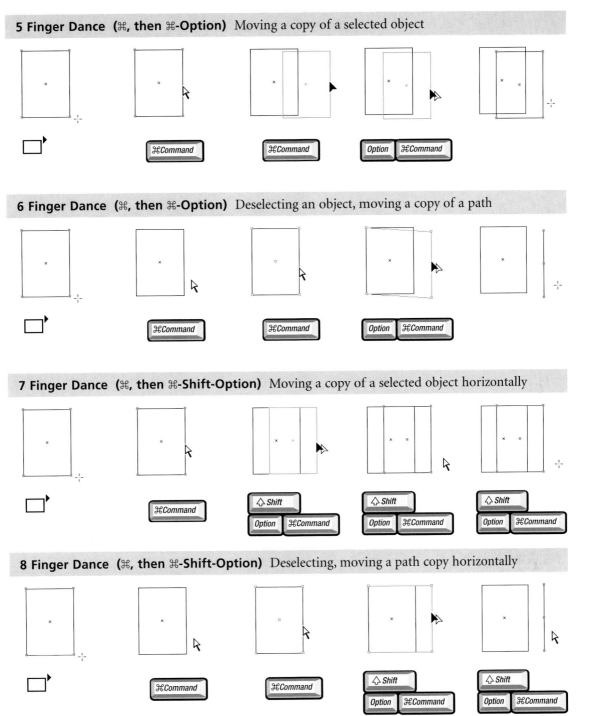

6 Finger Dance (⌘, then ⌘-Option) Deselecting an object, moving a copy of a path

7 Finger Dance (⌘, then ⌘-Shift-Option) Moving a copy of a selected object horizontally

8 Finger Dance (⌘, then ⌘-Shift-Option) Deselecting, moving a path copy horizontally

Note: *Before you begin this sequence of exercises, choose the Direct-selection tool, then select the Rectangle tool and drag to create a rectangle.*

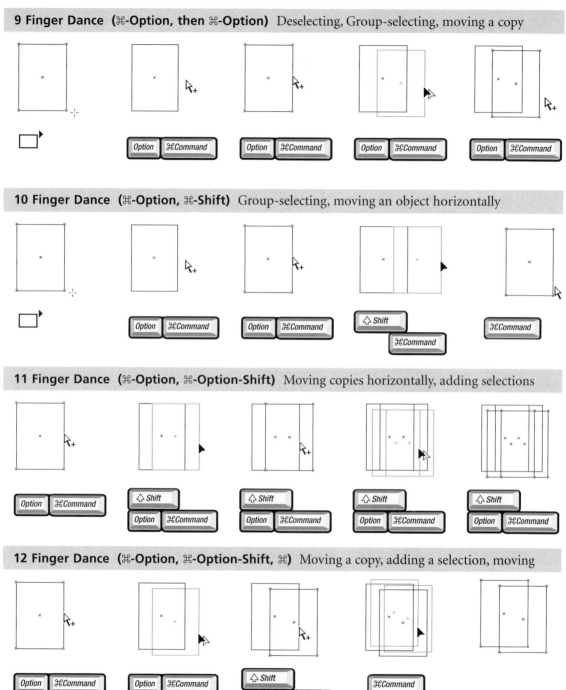

9 Finger Dance (⌘-Option, then ⌘-Option) Deselecting, Group-selecting, moving a copy

10 Finger Dance (⌘-Option, ⌘-Shift) Group-selecting, moving an object horizontally

11 Finger Dance (⌘-Option, ⌘-Option-Shift) Moving copies horizontally, adding selections

12 Finger Dance (⌘-Option, ⌘-Option-Shift, ⌘) Moving a copy, adding a selection, moving

Lines, Fills & Colors

3

Lines, Fills & Colors

Introduction…

Copying styles between files

To copy the style of an object in one document to an object in another document:

- Resize both document windows so the object you want to change is selected in the top window, and the object whose style you want to copy is visible, but in the window underneath.
- Just as you would ordinarily do with the Eyedropper tool, double-click on the object you want to copy (in the back window) to load its style into the selected object in the front window.

Eyedropper picks up *any* color!

With the Eyedropper, hold the mouse button, and drag *anywhere* (even the desktop!) to load colors into the Paint Style palette.

Customizing "style sheets"

Use the Eyedropper and Paint-bucket to create "style sheets," which can store stroke, line and color styles for each project. See Tip above and the techniques on pages 60 and 62 for creation and organizational suggestions.

Lines, fills and colors are at the core of creating with Adobe Illustrator. The Adobe manuals and tutorials explain the rudiments of constructing simple objects, so this chapter will instead focus on techniques for going beyond the basics. If you look carefully, you'll discover that virtually all the techniques in this chapter are used (as basics) in combination with some of the flashier techniques found in the chapters that follow.

Adobe Illustrator, mixed with a healthy dose of careful observation and attention to detail, can help you create quick, simple and elegant images without any of the fuss or muss of complex tricks or special effects.

Two cool Illustrator tools are the Eyedropper (which *picks up* line, fill and color styles) and the Paint-bucket (which *deposits* line, fill and color styles). While *Chapter 1* and Adobe's *User Guide* and *Tutorial* introduce you to the basics of working with palettes to control lines, fills and colors, these two tools offer some extremely useful shortcuts for copying styles from one object to another, or even to pick up color from any bitmapped image object. Click on an object with the Eyedropper to set the default styling for your next object, or click on an object with the Paint-bucket to fill it with the current styling.

My favorite use of the Eyedropper is to copy a style from one object to another. Select the object you would like to change, choose the Eyedropper tool, and double-click on an object with the style you like. *Voilà!* Your selected object is now styled to match the object that you double-clicked on, including dashes, line weights or custom fills. By default, both the Eyedropper and Paint-bucket tools copy the complete styling of an object, but double-clicking on either of the tools in the Toolbox allows you to customize the settings for both. Strangely, the settings that control what is deposited into an object when you *double-click* with the Eyedropper are the settings you have chosen for the *Paint-bucket*.

One of the aspects of Illustrator that seems mysterious to newcomers is the way that path lines end. I am the first to encourage you to work in Artwork mode, but you may discover someday that, although the lines seem to contact perfectly in Artwork mode, they visibly overlap in Preview. The solution is found in the lower section of the Paint Style palette, which you can display by choosing the full palette icon (from the upper right corner of the Paint Style palette).

By selecting one of the three Caps styles for your line endings, Illustrator lets you determine how the endpoints of your selected paths will look. The first (and default) choice is called a Butt-cap, which causes your path to stop at the end anchor point. Butt-caps are essential for creating exact placement of one path up against another. The middle choice is the Round-cap, which rounds the endpoint in a more "natural" manner. Round-caps are especially good for softening the effect of single lines or curves, making them appear slightly less harsh and computery. The final type is the Projecting-cap, which can extend lines and dashes half of the stroke weight beyond the end anchor point. You should also know that in addition to determining the appearance of path endpoints, Caps styles also affect the shapes of dashed lines.

You can also adjust the corners in an angled path if they appear too flat, or stick out too far behind the anchor points. The default Miter-join with a limit of 4 usually looks just fine, but if you want to round or bevel your corners, simply choose the Round or Bevel-joins. Each line weight has a particular Miter-limit at which the joins will switch from blunt to pointy; the thicker the line, the higher the limit will be. Miter-limits can range from 1 (which is always blunt) to 500.

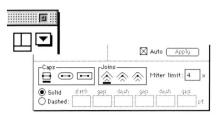

The full palette icon and the bottom section of the Paint Style palette

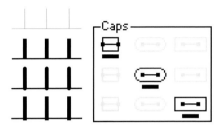

The same lines shown first in Artwork, then in Preview with Butt-caps, Round-caps and Projecting-caps

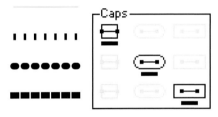

A 5-pt dashed line with a 2-pt dash and 6-pt gap shown first in Artwork, then Preview with a Butt-cap, Round-cap and Projecting-cap

A path shown first in Artwork, then in Preview with a Miter-join, Round-join and Bevel-join

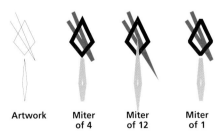

| Artwork | Miter of 4 | Miter of 12 | Miter of 1 |

Objects with 6-pt strokes and various Miter-limits, demonstrating that the angles of lines, as well as weight, affect Miter-limits

Filling open objects

Illustrator allows you to fill both closed *and* open objects (see page 114 for a practical example of filling open objects).

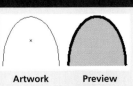

Artwork   Preview

Simply Realistic

Realism from Geometry and Observation

Overview: *Re-create a mechanical object using and altering the Rectangle or Oval tools; place all inner enclosed objects while finding the right values; add selected highlights and offset shadows and reflections.*

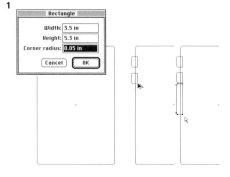

Creating and adjusting rounded rectangles to construct the basic forms

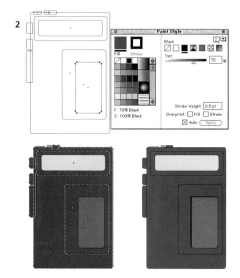

Filling objects with tints of black, stroked with a .5-pt, 100% black line

Many people believe the only way to achieve realism in Illustrator is with elaborate tricks of gradients and blends, but this illustration by Patrick Lynch proves that artistic observation is the real secret. For his *Manual of Ornithology* (with Noble S. Proctor, for Yale University Press), Lynch needed a few illustrations of equipment to aid in birdwatching, so he took the opportunity to learn Adobe Illustrator.

1 Re-creating a mechanical object with repeating geometric shapes and altering copies of objects to maintain regularity. You probably already know that close observation, and not complex perspective, is the most crucial aspect to rendering your illustration. And to focus your attention on the power of basic shapes, choose a simple mechanical device to render. Experiment with the Oval, Rectangle and Rounded Rectangle tools to place the basic elements. Especially with mechanical devices, components often tend to be similar; thus, look to where you can adjust a copy of an object, rather than create another that might not align perfectly. For his personal stereo/radio knobs, Lynch dragged a copy of one knob (holding down Shift-Option) and then stretched it by selecting one end with the Direct-selection tool and dragging it down (with the Shift key), creating a sequence of knobs with the same height, but different widths.

2 Using tints to fill the objects. Select all your objects and choose a .5-pt black stroke from the Paint Style palette. Then select an object (or set of objects), set the Fill to Black, and create a tint using the Tint slider. Continue to fill and adjust the tints for individual objects until you are happy with the basic value structure. Lynch used percentages from 10–80%, with the majority of the objects being 80% black.

3 Creating a few carefully placed highlights. Look closely at your object and decide where to place selected highlights. Start with a couple of thin, lighter-tinted lines, making sure to choose Round-caps for the lines (in the bottom section of the Paint palette). In a couple of instances, place shorter and slightly heavier lines of an even lighter tint on top of the first lines. For lines that follow the contour of your object, select part of your object's path with the Direct-selection tool and copy and Paste In Front that part of the path. Use your cursor-keys to offset the contour and use the Eyedropper to double-click on one of your highlight lines to set the contour with the highlight line style. If you need to trim contours, use the Scissors tool and delete the unwanted portion of the path. Lastly, using a light tint as a fill, with no stroke, create a small circle at the confluence of two lines (try leaving a small gap between the lines and the circle). Option-drag the circle if you wish to place it in other locations. For his highlights, Lynch used lines varying in weight from .5 to 2 points, in tints from 0 (white) to 50%, and five carefully placed white circles.

4 Creating shadows and transparencies. Follow the same procedure as above, but this time use darker tints to create shadows and transparencies. Make sure to offset shadows behind the object, especially if the shadows have solid fills. 🌑

Carefully placing a few lighter-tinted, filled circles and lines with Round-caps for highlights

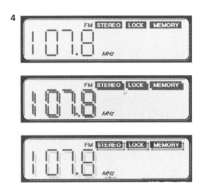

Creating text and LED numbers, then offsetting objects and giving offsets a darker gray tint

Making subtle changes in value to create the illusion of transparency

The Artwork view of the final illustration

Combining Circles
Cutting and Joining Overlapping Objects

Overview: *Design an illustration using overlapping objects; cut and remove overlaps and join objects.*

LINO BOY'S MOTTO: "I AM HIGHLY RESOLVED!"

1 ☐ Open this document as ──── ☐ Illustrator Template (PICT) │ OK │

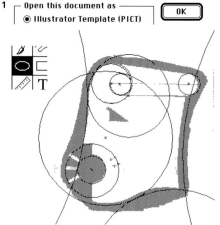

Using the Oval tool to trace circles over the PICT template

2

Selecting an object and locking everything else, then using the Scissors tool to cut overlaps

The first cut section, selecting pairs of anchors after moving the excess paths out of the way, then using ⌘-Option-J on the pair

Adobe Illustrator is a flexible enough program to accommodate many different illustration styles. Mark Fox has always designed using a compass to draw perfect circles, an unusual drawing style that translates easily to computer illustration. Use this technique to join any two objects, but don't forget also to look at filters (*Chapter 6*).

1 Placing your objects into the correct positions. Create your objects without worrying about how they overlap. Fox made a sketch with his compass, then scanned it and saved it as a PICT file. In Illustrator, Fox chose File: Open, located the PICT file and clicked OK to open it as a template (see *Chapter 4* for template help). Holding down the Shift key, Fox traced circles with the Oval tool.

2 Cropping the objects, removing the excess and joining the objects. Select one object, hold down the Option key and choose Arrange: Lock (⌘-Option-1) to lock everything else. With the Scissors tool, click on the path where this object will overlap and join with others. Then choose Arrange: Unlock All (⌘-2) and repeat for the other objects. Finally, with the Direct-selection tool, move the extra paths you cut out of the way, select a pair of points you want to join, and press ⌘-Option-J to average and join them in one step. Repeat until you have joined all your objects. ✏️

Gallery: Mark Fox / BlackDog

Mark Fox's whimsical design style hasn't visibly changed since his transition from ink and compass to Adobe Illustrator. The sketch to the right above for "Horse of a Different Color" shows Fox's notations for compass centers, as well as the circles. Although most people rely primarily on the Pen tool when drawing in Illustrator, Fox creates all his logos by cutting and joining rectangles and circles—occasionally using the Pen tool (for straight lines) and the Rotate tool.

A Variety of Lines

Overlapping Lines to Form Roads and Rails

Overview: *Use sequences of Copy and Paste In Front to create variations in line styles to form highways and railroads.*

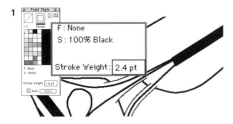

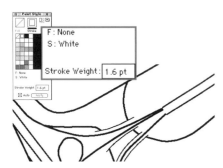

The black outline and white knockout styles

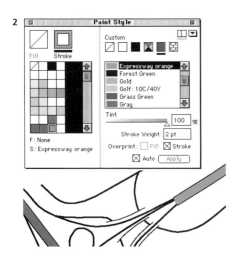

Custom colors can also be dragged and stored as swatches in the left palette

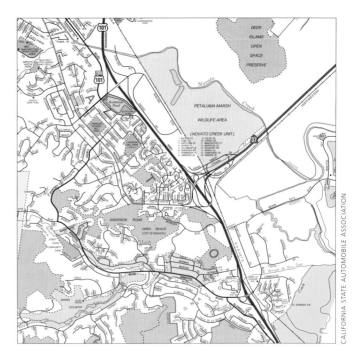

You can create many special effects by varying line styles (see "Dashed Lines" in Illustrator's *Beyond the Basics* guide). The California State Automobile Association (CSAA) uses overlapping line styles in its road maps to represent streets, highways and even railroad tracks.

1 Creating the black outline and the white "knockout." Using the Pen tool, create curves or lines and choose the View: Preview mode so you can work in color. Select all the objects you wish to convert into road map highways (see the *Glossary* for object selection suggestions), open the Paint Style palette and style these first paths with no fill and a wide, 2.4-pt black stroke. Keep the paths selected, although you can use View: Hide Edges (⌘-Shift-H) to hide (or show) the path selection lines as you work.

Copy the selected objects and choose Edit: Paste In Front (⌘-F) to paste a copy exactly on top of the original objects. Change the copied objects to a white, 1.6-pt stroke, which will automatically "knock out" colors underneath in the printing process.

2 Pasting another copy in front and styling it in a color. The next step is again to choose Edit: Paste In Front, style this copy in a color at a 2-pt line weight and check Overprint in the palette, which allows for a .2-pt trap between the black outline and white knockout.

3 Pasting a final black line down the center of the highway. To create the dividing lines on the highway, use ⌘-F to paste another copy in front and style the line with a black, .4-pt stroke.

4 Creating the black line for the railroad, then pasting a dashed-line copy in front for railroad ties. Create a new curve or line and set the stroke to .3-pt black. The crossties will be created by overlaying this original with a 3-pt dashed line. With the .3-pt line selected, choose Copy, then ⌘-F. Give this line a stroke of 3 points and open the Paint Style palette fully to reveal the bottom section (click on the bottom horizontal portion of the little palette icon in the upper right corner or hold down on the arrow to select the icon representing all three palette sections). In the bottom section of the palette, click on the button labeled "Dashed." To create the railroad crossties, click in the first text box labeled "dash" (this creates the solid portion of the dash), type ".3" (meaning points) and use the Tab key to move to the next text field to specify a gap of 14. Press Return or click outside the palette to apply the final changes. If you want to re-enter new numbers, make sure your cursor is actively blinking in the text box before you type. 💿

Overprinting blacks and knocking out whites
Although the Paint Style palette allows you to check "Overprint" when you assign any fill or stroke, choose Filter: Colors: Overprint Blacks to specify global parameters for overprinting blacks (choose Filter: Other in Illustrator 5). Remember, whenever you use white it automatically knocks out all colors underneath.

Using macros for auto-styling
Try out Alien Skin's Stylist (in the *Wow!* disk's Plug-ins folder) for multi-path style "Constructions."

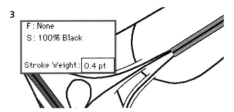

3

The black line down the center of the highway

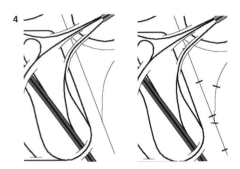

4

The railroad base alone and the crosstie dashes

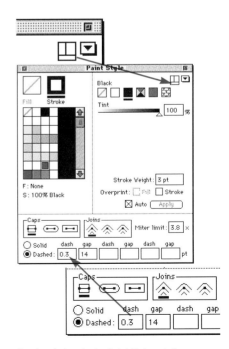

Setting dashes in the Paint Style palette

Isometric Systems

Cursor-keys, Constrain-angles & Formulas

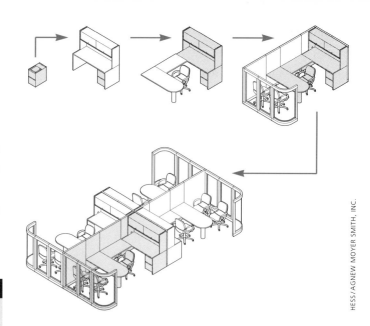

HESS / AGNEW MOYER SMITH, INC.

Overview: *Create detailed views of an object from front, top and side; use an isometric formula to transform the objects; set "Constrain-angle" and "Cursor key" distance; use cursor-keys with snap-to-point to adjust and assemble objects.*

Stubborn snapping-to-point

Sometimes if you try to move an object over slightly, it will annoyingly "snap" to the wrong place. If this happens, move it away from the area and release. Then regrab the object at the point from which you'd like to align it and move it so that it snaps into the correct position. If you still have trouble, zoom in. As a last resort, you can disable "Snap to point" in General Preferences.

1

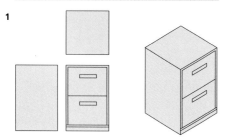

Separate views, then after transformations

2

Scaling, skewing and rotating

Technical illustrations and diagrams are often depicted in isometric perspective, and Adobe Illustrator can be the ideal program both for creating your initial illustrations and for transforming them into this perspective. The artists at Agnew Moyer Smith (AMS) created and transformed the diagrams on these pages using their three-step perspective. For both the initial creation and manipulation of the isometric objects in space, AMS custom-set "Cursor key distance" and "Constrain angle," and made sure that "Snap to point" was enabled—all from General Preferences.

1 Creating detailed renderings of the front, side and top views of your object to scale. Before you begin a technical illustration, you should choose a drawing scale, then coordinate the settings in General Preferences to match. For instance, to create a file drawer in the scale of 1 mm = 2", set the ruler units to millimeters and "Cursor key" distance to .5 mm, and make sure that the "Snap to point" option is enabled. With these features enabled and matching your drawing scale, it's easy to create detailed views of your object. With your ruler units set to the correct scale, choose Window: Show Info to keep easy track of your object sizing as you work. If a portion of the real object is inset 1" to the left, you can use the ← cursor-key to move the path one increment (.5 mm) further left. Finally, snap to point will help you properly fit together and assemble your various components. Select and group all the components of the front view. Separately group the top and side so you'll be able to easily isolate each of the views for transformation and assembly. AMS renders every internal detail, which allows them to view "cutaways" or adjust individual elements, or groups of elements, such as opening a drawer.

2 Using an isometric formula to transform your viewpoints. The artists at AMS created and transformed the diagrams on these pages using their three-step process, which is fully demonstrated on the *Wow!* disk. To transform your objects, double-click on the various tools to specify the correct percentages numerically. First, select all three views and scale them 100% horizontally and 86.6% vertically. Next, select the top and side, shearing them at a −30° angle, and then shear the front 30°. Lastly, rotate the top and front 30° and the side −30°.

3 Assembling the top, front and side. With the Selection tool, grab a specific anchor-point from the side view that will contact the front view, and drag it until it snaps into the correct position (the arrow turns hollow). Next, select and drag to snap the top into position. Finally, select and group the entire object for easy reselection.

4 Using the constrain-angle and cursor-keys to adjust objects and assemble multiple components. Look at the Movement chart to determine the direction in which to move. Try using the Direct-selection tool to select a portion of the object, setting the constrain-angle to 30° (or −30°), then using the ← and → cursor-keys to slide your selection along that isometric axis. Or, use the Selection tool to select entire objects and snap them into position against other objects. 🌀

4

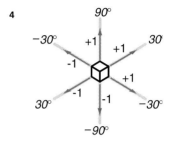

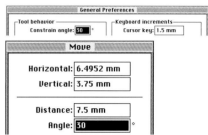

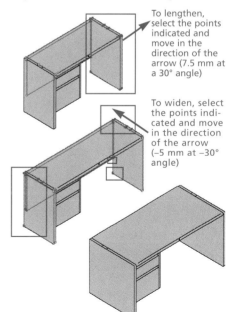

To lengthen, select the points indicated and move in the direction of the arrow (7.5 mm at a 30° angle)

To widen, select the points indicated and move in the direction of the arrow (−5 mm at −30° angle)

Transforming one object into the next, by Direct-selecting the appropriate anchor points and using the Move command, or by setting and using custom constrain-angle and cursor-keys

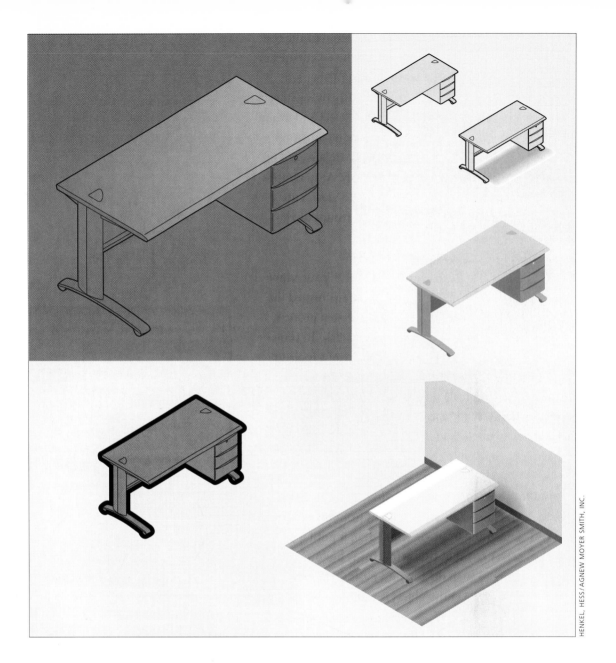

Gallery: Rick Henkel, Kurt Hess / Agnew Moyer Smith, Inc.

Creating a technical illustration in Illustrator may save you time over traditional graphic methods, but the real time savings lies in producing variations on a theme. Agnew Moyer Smith's artists use Illustrator because it provides so much flexibility in altering an illustration after construction of objects is complete. These different presentations of desks for Steelcase office furniture demonstrate how dramatically different the visual effect can be just by altering the stroke and fill styles of an object and its immediate surroundings. The shadow on the wood floor was set to the Overprint option.

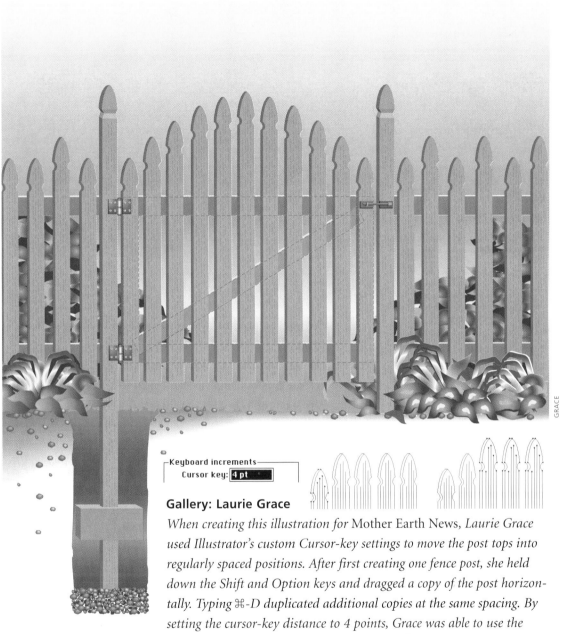

Keyboard increments
Cursor key: `4 pt`

Gallery: Laurie Grace

When creating this illustration for Mother Earth News, *Laurie Grace used Illustrator's custom Cursor-key settings to move the post tops into regularly spaced positions. After first creating one fence post, she held down the Shift and Option keys and dragged a copy of the post horizontally. Typing ⌘-D duplicated additional copies at the same spacing. By setting the cursor-key distance to 4 points, Grace was able to use the Direct-selection tool to select the top portion of the first post and then the ↓ cursor-key twice to move the post down 8 points. She could then use the Direct-selection tool to select all the top sections except for the first two posts and move them up with the ↑ cursor-key. Deselecting the left post, Grace could continue to move the remaining posts up. She could continue to move one or more posts at a time, and at the end, set the cursor-key distance smaller for making slight visual adjustments to create the proper arc at the top of the fence.*

Customizing Color
Custom Labels for Making Quick Changes

Overview: *Define custom colors; type labels for the colors; select and edit colors and objects.*

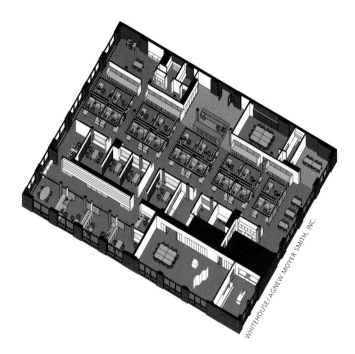

1

Creating a custom color

2
Wood Floor

A typed custom label

Wood Floor
Wood Floor

Setting the typestyle to a thin, black outline with the correct custom fill; and the final typed label at actual size

When you need to store dozens of color swatches, it is essential to develop a method to organize the colors. Designers at Agnew Moyer Smith (AMS) invented a clever system using custom colors to label different categories of objects, allowing the designers to isolate and change the custom colors easily, as well as enabling them to make global changes to any category of objects filled with a given custom color.

1 Creating custom colors. Many ways to create custom colors exist in Illustrator, and perhaps one of the easiest is just to choose Custom Color from the Object menu. Click New, and you will have the opportunity to name your color. In this case, give your color a name that will signify the type of object you plan to fill with the color. Then use the process color sliders to create the correct mix of CMYK for printing. Bob Whitehouse of AMS used labels such as "Wood Floor," "Computer" and "Window Frame" to label the colors he wished to use in his illustration above. To help in the selection of reliably reproduceable colors, Whitehouse used the Agfa *PostScript Process Color Guide* to look up the color he actually wanted and then entered the percentages of CMYK indicated in the book. (For more about color consistency, see page 21.)

2 Typing a label for each of the colors. After you have created a custom color, use the Type tool to type a label for the color on the side of your illustration. If you want the labels to print, place the type within the page margins. If you don't want the labels to print, then place the type outside the margins. Choose a selection tool and click on the text block if necessary to activate the baseline of the type. Open the Paint Style palette so the right side is visible (see "Working With Palettes," page 14, for help). To make the label useful, style it identically to the objects to be created using the like-named custom color. For instance, for the label "Wood Floor," Whitehouse chose a .33-pt, black stroke and filled the type with the custom color "Wood Floor."

3 Repeating the procedure for all colors and labels. Create colors for each object to be styled differently, and make labels for all your custom colors. Whitehouse needed to create dozens of custom colors, properly labeled, for each type of object included in his floor plan.

4 Changing color definitions as necessary. The custom color system makes it easy to change definitions of colors. From the Paint Style palette, double-click on the color you want to change to open the Custom Color dialog box, where you can make changes to the color recipes. Click OK to apply the changes to all objects containing that color.

5 Using the labels to find all like objects. To find all like objects, for instance, "Wood Beams," click on the name in your list and choose Filter: Select: Same Paint Style to select all wood beams in your illustration. Once selected, you can reposition or recolor them all together. ✐

Close-up and zoomed-out views of the illustration with the labels

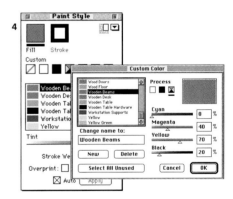

Double-clicking on a custom color swatch in the Paint Style palette to open its dialog box

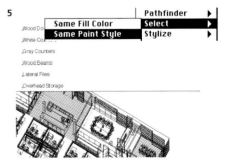

Selecting the label, then using the Select: Same Paint Style filter to find the objects

Organizing Color
Arranging an Artist's Palette of Colors

Overview: *Work with color swatches to choose initial colors; make adjustments to, and rename, custom colors; save a palette of your custom colors.*

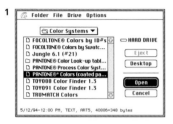

Importing the Pantone color model

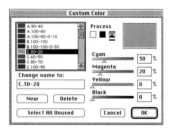

Respecifying and renaming custom colors to form an orderly, accessible palette

Moving multiple sliders

With the Shift key down, if you grab one of the color sliders you'll move all colors together. Drag to the right to 100% to saturate the color fully for easy tinting. Drag left to desaturate.

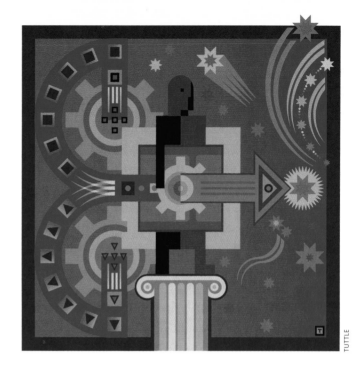

TUTTLE

As any colorist knows, a well-organized palette can go beyond providing you with mere colors; it can facilitate the creative process. Progress Software Company's product signature color is the deep Pantone Violet #2685, so when art director Deborah Hurst commissioned artist Jean Tuttle to create a series of illustrations for a "family" of Progress sales literature, they worked closely to develop a limited palette that would feel related to the signature color. Tuttle developed a method to organize the colors so she could work with them in an intuitive manner.

1 Using swatches of printed colors to choose ranges of colors with which to work. As I mentioned in *Chapter 1*, color on the computer is not a reliable predictor of the color you will get in print. Therefore, start with one of the computer-to-print color matching systems to choose your initial colors. With art director Hurst in Boston, and Tuttle in Dobbs Ferry, New York, the two used the Pantone color system to discuss and choose swatches of color to consider for the palette. Once they had agreed upon the general color scheme, Tuttle could open the Pantone color document and gain access to the computer version of the colors from within Illustrator (see "Importing colors and styles," page 23, for help). For each color that she was considering, Tuttle put a square filled with that color into a document she called "RDBMS Palette" (which refers to the Progress product). After she pulled the basic colors she wanted, she could close the Pantone document—leaving her with just the colors she had chosen for her palette.

Opening the Custom Colors dialog box, Tuttle re-named each color based on five color groupings: Blues, Purples, Blue Violets, Red Violets and Accents. Because Illustrator lists custom colors alphabetically, Tuttle pre-ceded each color grouping by a letter that would force Illustrator to group the colors as she wished. Using a process color matching book as a guide, Tuttle then rounded off the CMYK percentages for each individual color, incorporating the color formulas in the name (B.50-50, for example, would be Purples: 50% Cyan/50% Magenta) and created variants on each of the colors as well, saving each color swatch into her palette. To visually separate the color groupings as they list in the Paint Style palette, she created a series of white colors to use purely as name placeholders—for example, one white was named "B. Purples" (because there's a space before the "P," it lists ahead of the numbered purples in the list)—making sure that each of these white custom colors used as a label was placed into a square in the palette as well.

2 Accessing and tinting colors with your palette.
Another benefit to using custom colors in your palette is that you can easily specify tint percentages for any color. Just select the color and adjust the Tint slider below or type in a percentage in the text box alongside. For each illustration that Tuttle produced for the Progress series, she had access to her entire set of colors and their tints. With this palette, Tuttle was able to create a "smoky blue" color environment that she could use for the entire family of illustrations. ☺

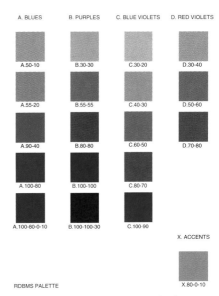

A chart made of the custom colors for future access to the full palette, including a rectangle for each white made as a name placeholder

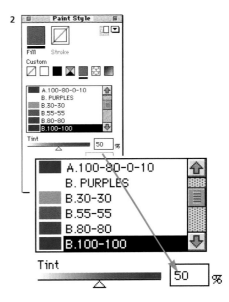

Specifying a tint of a custom color

Tints will "stick" until changed
The tint percentages of your last selected object will set the tint of your next fill and stroke color, unless you manually change them.

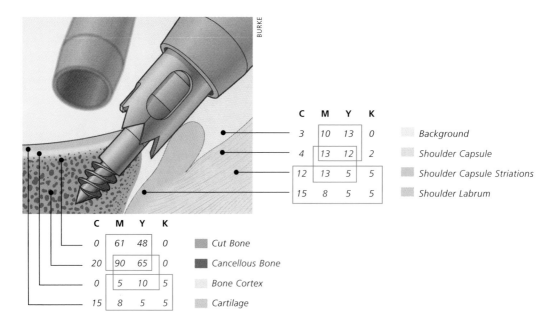

Gallery: Christopher Burke

When printed using the CMYK four-color process, Adobe Illustrator's smooth, crisp edges can be a registration nightmare. Even the slightest misregistration of inks can create visually disturbing white gaps between colors. So, although you shouldn't have to worry about what happens to your illustration once it's completed, the reality is that in this phase of computer graphics evolution, you still have to help your printer along. "Trapping" is a technique of printing one color over the edge of another—usually achieved by creating overprinting strokes that overlap adjacent objects. However, work-around solutions exist; Christopher Burke, for example, constructs the colors in his images in such a way as to ensure "continuous coverage" for at least one (preferably two) of the color plates in every region of his image. As long as adjacent objects share at least 5% of at least one color, no white gaps can form, and trapping will naturally occur! (See also the tips below and on page 21.) This method of keeping just enough in common between adjacent colors allows Burke to maintain a full-spectrum palette. (The background of the image above is an Illustrator drawing rasterized in Photoshop and placed back into Illustrator as an EPS—see Chapter 4 *for placing EPS images, and* Chapter 9 *for more on rasterizing Illustrator images.)*

Manual trapping of gradients and pattern fills

Since you can't style strokes with gradients or patterns, you can't trap using the Pathfinder Trap filter either. To trap gradients and patterns manually, first duplicate your object and stroke it in the weight you'd like for a trap. Then use Filter: Objects: Outline Path to convert the stroke to a filled object, which you should fill in the same style as the object you'd like to trap. Lastly, enable the Overprint Fill box in the Paint Style palette. If necessary, use the Gradient-fill tool to unify gradients across objects (page 108), and manually replicate pattern transformations.

Gallery: Dorothy Remington / Remington Designs

Color printers are notoriously unpredictable in terms of color consistency, so Dorothy Remington developed a method to increase consistency from proof to final output. When Remington constructs an image, she freely chooses colors from any of the CMYK process color models (Pantone Process, TruMatch, Focoltone and Toyo) that come with Illustrator, provided that she has the matching color swatchbooks. When she sends the computer file to the service bureau for proofing, as well as for final output, she also sends along the color swatches representing colors used in the image. Remington asks the service bureau to calibrate the printer to match the enclosed swatches as closely as possible. Although requesting such special attention might result in a small surcharge, it can save you an immense amount of time (in back-and-forths to the service bureau) and expense in reprinting the image because colors did not turn out as expected.

Gallery: Hugh Whyte / Lehner & Whyte

To celebrate Letraset's distribution of a new Pantone line of blacks, Hugh Whyte was commissioned to produce a thematic illustration for Letraset to silk-screen on T-shirts. The beauty of using the Pantone custom colors was that when he had them printed to positive separations, the films were perfectly registered for the different screens in silk-screening. The printer could then mix the inks to Whyte's exact specifications using the Pantone swatchbook to match.

BARNEY / BARNEY MCKAY DESIGN

Gallery: Jeffrey Barney / Barney McKay Design

When Santa Anita Park decided to produce a commemorative poster, Jeffrey Barney chose this 1930s-style illustration to reflect the park's period elegance. The color proofs needed to match the actual colors used at the park, to be of large enough format to view at near poster size, and to be consistent with the colors that would result from the printing process. Given these parameters, Barney decided to calibrate all of his work against Iris prints (see the Resource Index*). He therefore had his computer monitors professionally calibrated to match the prints. He also regularly brought the prints to the park and made color notes directing himself how to alter each color. In Illustrator, Barney created a set of custom colors labeled by name, so as he adjusted the CMYK formula for each color, all occurrences of that color would automatically update, as well as all the corresponding tints. (For more on tints, see page 62.) Finally, after proofing the final Iris prints, the service bureau matched the color separations to them.*

Brush Strokes

Making Realistic Marks with the Brush

Overview: *Set the Brush tool to the desired range of widths; trace or draw your composition; select and group brush drawing; optionally, make a slightly different version to copy and paste on top of the original; make final adjustments.*

1

The original sketch in red Conté crayon

The PICT scan opened as an Illustrator template

Creating spontaneous painterly and calligraphic marks is a wonderful recent addition to Illustrator. As long as you have a graphics tablet and a pressure-sensitive, pen-like stylus, Illustrator's Brush tool can literally sense the pressure you apply and vary your strokes accordingly. For this portrait of Gregory Sloan Jacoby, I was able to use Illustrator's Brush tool with Wacom's ArtZ tablet to create a loose, brush-and-ink style, limited edition print.

1 If you'll be working from a source, prepare your template. Although you can draw directly into the computer, if you want to trace a sketch or a photograph, you'll need to prepare your template. For Gregory's portrait, I used AppleScan software to scan a 4" x 6" tight sketch at 400% at 75 pixels per inch and opened it as a template in Illustrator. (See *Chapter 4* for template help.)

2 Setting your brush preferences and drawing. Instead of actually creating painterly lines, Illustrator's Brush tool creates filled objects that appear to be variable weight lines. So unless you're experimenting with effects, set a solid color fill in the Paint Style palette with no stroke.

Double-click on the Brush tool to open the Brush Preferences dialog box. Experiment with the different settings until you find ranges that are comfortable for you. (Unfortunately, if you don't have a pressure-sensitive tablet, your brush stroke options will be limited.) Then draw. Make adjustments to colors or brush preferences as necessary. For Gregory's portrait, I initially worked with rather large strokes, so in the Brush Preferences box, I used a range of 1 to 6 points, with Round-caps and -joins (similar in concept to the Caps and Joins, page 49). **Note:** *With the Freehand tool, lowering the Freehand tolerance settings in General Preferences results in more points; higher results in fewer. This adjusting doesn't seem to affect the Brush tool.*

3 Cleaning up extra points. Objects created with the Brush tool will always need some cleaning up. The more extra points and oddly positioned points you have, the more irregular the image will appear when printed and the longer the image will take to print (some objects with too many points might not even print at all). Use the Delete-anchor-point tool to remove excess points interfering with the smoothness of curves, and use the Direct-selection tool to adjust the placement of anchor points and direction of curves.

4 Experimenting with your image. The first portrait I completed looked too clean, so I saved the version and kept experimenting with making slight adjustments using the Direct-selection tool to redraw a few of the lines. Since I liked parts of both versions, I selected and grouped each (⌘-G), then tried to combine the two, accidentally creating an offset that I liked. The softer brush effect in the final image is a result of this offset. 🖎

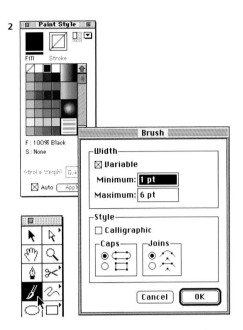

Setting Paint Style to fill, with no stroke, and double-clicking the Brush tool to set options

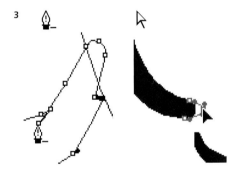

Eliminating extra points with the Delete-anchor-point tool and adjusting curves with the Direct-selection tool

Pasting a second, slightly altered version over the first version

Gallery: Lyuda Lavrentyeva

Lyuda Lavrentyeva used the Brush tool with a pressure-sensitive tablet and the Pantone NEC color matching system to create this loose, vivid image. Her working method incorporates many techniques demonstrated elsewhere in the book, such as creating the darker line drawing on a locked upper layer while adding the broad patches of color underneath (see page 84). Lavrentyeva also used a number of filters, including Pathfinder: Soft to blend colors, Pathfinder: Unite to join objects, and the Select: Select Same Fill filter to help her make global color changes. (See Chapter 6 *for more on filters, including the Stylize: Calligraphy filter.)*

Gallery: Jen Alspach

For this natural, ink-pen-like Illustrator drawing, Jen Alspach used the Wacom ArtZ tablet to trace one of her scanned horse photos (placed as an EPS custom template; see page 86). Alspach used a number of different tools to create a diversity of line texture, beginning with the Brush tool's Calligraphic option set to 120 to trace over the photo. After deleting the EPS template, she switched the Brush tool to a variable line weight between .5 and 3 to form some of the contouring lines, set the Freehand tool at 1, .5 and .125 to create the scratchy texture, and set the Brush tool's Calligraphic option at 45. Finally, Alspach created blends to complete the background (see Chapter 5*).*

MORENO

Gallery: Cheryl Moreno

With just pen and ink, Cheryl Moreno's delightful figures and "doodles" jump off the page. Until recently, Moreno would carefully use Illustrator's Pen tool to trace her spontaneously drawn calligraphic figures. Now that she has discovered the Brush tool and a Wacom tablet, Moreno is able to eliminate the sketch-and-scan phase.

MORENO

Intricate Patterns

Designing Complex Repeating Patterns

Advanced Technique

Overview: *Design a rough composi-tion; define a pattern boundary and place behind everything; use the box to define guides; place small lines to use as registration while dragging; define and use the pattern.*

1

Arranging objects into a basic design

Placing a confining rectangle (defining the pattern tile), guides and registration lines

Retrieving patterns

In the Objects: Patterns dialog box is an option to Paste a selected pattern; this option literally pastes a copy of the original objects creating that pattern into your current image window. (See page 76 for a practical use of this feature.)

Included with Illustrator are many wonderful patterns for you to use and customize, and the *User Guide* does a good job of explaining pattern-making basics. But what if you want to create a more complex pattern?

A few simple guidelines and registration marks can help you minimize what could be a painstaking process of trial and error. After many hours of designing and some essential help from trainer/consultant Sandee Cohen, I was finally able to come up with a method that allowed me to design experimentally an intricate tile that would print properly as a repeating pattern. This fabric and wallpaper pattern was created for an upcoming children's book I'm illustrating for writer Matt Lake.

1 Designing your basic pattern, then drawing a confining rectangle and guides. Create a design that will allow for some rearrangement of the elements. Be aware that you cannot make a pattern tile from objects filled with gradients, placed EPS images or other patterns. Use the Rectangle tool to draw a box around the part of the image you would like to repeat. This rectangle defines the boundary of the pattern tile. Send the rectangle to the back of the page or to the bottom drawing layer (if you would like help with layers, see *Chapter 4*). This boundary rectangle, which controls how your pattern repeats, *must* remain an unstroked, unfilled, nonrotated, nonskewed *rectangle*. Next, make sure that the "Snap to point" option is enabled (in General Preferences), then choose Show Rulers and pull out the guides to snap to each side of the rectangle (your cursor turns hollow as it snaps). Make sure you've selected the Lock Guides option (see pages 20 and 96 for more on guides).

Next, you need to create small lines that will help you to move objects while maintaining registration. On each of the guides, use the Pen tool to draw the lines outside of the pattern in a color not used in the pattern. These registration marks will help you to align elements as you move them from corner to corner.

2 Developing the repeating elements. In order for the pattern to repeat properly, you must place copies of any elements extending beyond the bounding rectangle in the area butting up against the overlapping object. For instance, if an object extends below the rectangle, you must place a copy of the continuing part of the object into the upper portion of the pattern. So, for the grass in the jungle pattern to repeat properly, I selected grass in front of the tiger and used Group (⌘-G) for easy reselection. In order to align the grass properly, I selected the bottom right horizontal registration mark with the grass that was to be moved. I grabbed the registration mark, and then, while holding down the Option and Shift keys (the Option key leaves the original, while the Shift constrains the dragging to vertical and horizontal movements), dragged a copy until it snapped into position along the upper horizontal guide. If you make a mistake, try again. (See "A Finger Dance" in *Chapter 2* for practice with Shift, Option and other modifier keys.)

3 Weaving your repeating objects in front of or behind others. One way to make a pattern interesting is to weave elements on top of some objects and behind

2
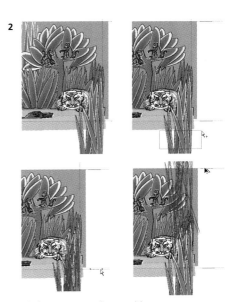
Moving grasses up into position

3
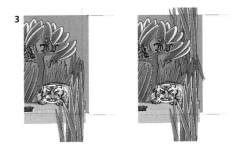
Cutting the copied grass and using Paste In Front to place it in front of the sky

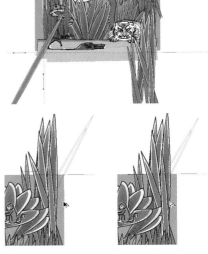
Weaving diagonal grasses through the pattern

4

others. After you've placed your copy of the repeating element into its properly registered position, and while it is still selected, cut the copy to the Clipboard (⌘-X). Then choose an object or objects in your composition that you can easily Paste In Front of (⌘-F) or Paste In Back of (⌘-B) other objects. For the jungle, I cut the grass copy, then selected the blue sky and chose Paste In Front, which placed the copy in front of the blue sky but behind all other elements. Other grasses, such as the diagonal blades, needed to be on top of some grass while behind others. I used a combination of Paste In Front and Paste In Back with such elements to increase the complexity of the weaving.

4 **Testing your pattern.** When you're ready to test your pattern (to see if you like what you've done so far), make sure that all the objects and layers you need are visible and unlocked (⌘-4, ⌘-2), then select your pattern elements, including the bounding rectangle. To create the pattern, choose Object: Pattern and click New (if your backmost selected object isn't a rectangle, you'll get an error message reminding you to select one). You should see a small preview of your pattern tile. If you like what you see, click OK; if you don't, click Cancel. Once you've prepared the tile to your liking, create a new object and fill it with your new pattern; in the right side of your Paint Style palette, click on the pattern icon, then find and select your new pattern from the list.

Controlling patterns

To adjust how a pattern repeats, "Transform pattern tiles" in General Preferences must be enabled. To manually move, rotate, scale or skew the pattern tile, start your transformation and hold down the "P" key as you drag (or use the cursor-keys). You can also transform patterns in any of the dialog boxes (with or without the object itself). Once you transform a pattern, new objects will copy those transformations, until you "re-zero" the settings by choosing a non-pattern. Relocate the ruler origin to set where the next pattern will begin. For more about patterns, Path Patterns and Expanding patterns into editable objects, see ❻ and page 76.

5 **Simplifying and scaling your final pattern.** The larger and more complex your pattern is, the more difficult and time-consuming it will be to print. When you finally get a pattern you like, do your best to minimize its size. (If you used the Paint tool, see page 68, this chapter, for deleting excess points; see *Chapter 6* for filters that can simplify your piece.) Finally, with only your current window open, from the Pattern dialog box, select unused patterns and delete them. Make sure you save this smallest possible version of your file with a new name. ◐

STEUER

Gallery: Sharon Steuer

A reduced version of the final pattern (tile prescaled to 52%). In the original pattern tile, I used the Brush tool (see pages 68 through 71), multiple layers to separate the colored elements (see Chapter 4), and the Blend tool (see Chapter 5) to create the color transitions in the sky and leaves.

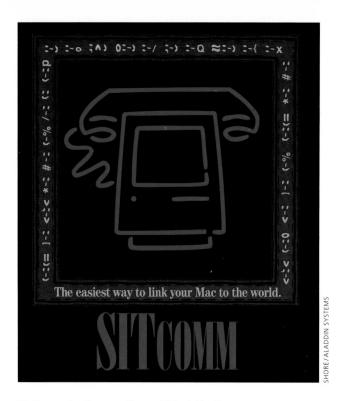

The easiest way to link your Mac to the world.

SITCOMM

2 repeats of the border shown at actual size for the T-shirt

The Adobe "Primitives" pattern that was customized for the SITcomm border

Gallery: Anthony Shore / Aladdin Systems

Initial sketches by Cindy Briggs inspired Anthony Shore to create a unique T-shirt design by modifying one of Adobe's "Primitives" patterns. Instead of using the pattern itself, Shore used the objects that formed the pattern (to select objects used in any pattern, choose Paste from Objects: Pattern) and adjusted them to appear irregular by using Filter: Roughen (see Chapter 6 and page 168), and the Direct-selection tool. For the faces within the border, Shore created type elements inspired by Seth Godin's Smiley Dictionary, transforming them into outlines (see page 138). He styled the faces using Pantone PMS 123 Gold with a 1.5-pt overprinting gold stroke as a trap against the PMS Violet. The final design, on a white background, was color-separated and printed on a black T-shirt.

Herbal Carpet & Household Freshener

Net Wt. 16 oz. .45 kg.

CLEAN & GREEN
ECOLOGICAL HOME CARE ™

Gallery: Anita Soos Design

The User Guide *can help you create simple repeating patterns. For each product in the "Clean & Green" line, Kim Zolvik of Anita Soos Design customized one of Adobe's commercial patterns. For this carpet freshener packaging, Zolvik altered the Adobe "Leaves-Matisse" pattern.*

Templates & Layers

4

Templates & Layers

When work arrived from over 70 of the country's Illustrator experts, it seemed that very few artists were actually using layers for tasks beyond isolating text as an overlay above an image. However, as this chapter exemplifies, some artists *have* found innovative ways to use layers to simplify and enhance the Illustrator working environment significantly.

Layers themselves are quite easy to use, once you're in the habit. One of the beautiful aspects of Illustrator's implementation of multiple layers is that you cannot move objects to locked or hidden layers. That might seem like an unnecessary restraint, but in Aldus FreeHand the opposite approach results in objects mysteriously disappearing into hidden layers.

Though the Layers palette is a relatively new addition, Illustrator has always provided a powerful and flexible drawing environment to manage the stacking order of objects. The seemingly straightforward commands Hide, Show, Lock, Unlock (from the Arrange menu), and Paste In Front and Paste In Back (from the Edit menu) offer considerable control over Illustrator objects. Even though you can now benefit fully from the newer layers functions discussed at length in this chapter, the original secret powers are still well worth learning:

Paste In Front, Paste In Back (⌘-F, ⌘-B)
Even if you use a million layers to separate objects, you will *still* need these two functions. They don't merely paste an object in front of or behind all other objects; they paste *exactly* in front of or behind the object you select. The second, and equally important, aspect is that the two functions paste objects that are cut (⌘-X) or copied (⌘-C) in the exact same location (in relation to the page margins). This ability applies from one document to another, ensuring perfect registration and alignment when you copy and use Paste In Front/Back. These

Showing and unlocking layers

Layers palette basics:

- A dot under the Eye means a layer is visible; a dot under the Pencil means it's unlocked.

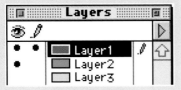

- Click to place dots in, or remove them from, the Eye or Pencil columns. Or, click-drag up and down to remove dots or place them in multiple layers.
- Double-click on a layer to open that layer's print and view preferences.
- Shift-click to select multiple layers, then let go of the Shift key. When multiple layers are selected, if you then click on the Eye or Pencil itself, you will hide/lock all layers that are not selected. Double-clicking on one layer will access Preferences, which you can set for all the selected layers.

To select *all* objects

Unlock and show all layers (⌘-2), unlock and show all objects, (⌘-4), *then* press ⌘-A (Select All).

functions apply only when the "Paste remembers layers" option in General Preferences is *disabled*—see "Layer Registration" later in this chapter for the practical application of checking this option. (The *Wow!* disk includes exercises on reordering objects using pasting and layers.)

Lock (⌘-1) / Unlock All (⌘-2)

When you're trying to select an object, and you accidentally select an object on top of it, try locking the selected object and clicking again. Repeat as necessary until you reach the correct object. When you're done with the task at hand, choose ⌘-2 to Unlock All.

Warning: You can use the Direct-selection tool to select and lock objects that are part of a group (see page 9 for more on grouping)—but if you select an unlocked object in the group with the Group-select or other selection tools, the locked objects can become selected, making it too easy for them to be transformed accidentally or even deleted. Hidden objects, of course, will stay hidden even if you select other objects in the same group.

Hide (⌘-3) / Show All (⌘-4)

An alternate approach for handling objects that get in the way is to select them and choose ⌘-3, which hides them. To use Show All on hidden objects, choose ⌘-4.

Note: *Hidden objects won't print but may reappear if you export them to other programs, or upon reopening.*

Templates

One of the layer substitutes that Illustrator has always provided is the Template layer, and this chapter reveals some ways to use the template optimally, as well as how to bypass the template for higher-resolution tracing.

Taking advantage of Unlock All and Show All

After use of Show All or Unlock All, objects that were hidden or locked will appear selected. While they're selected, you can deselect specific objects (Shift-Direct-select), then relock or hide the objects still selected.

If you can't select an object...

If you have trouble selecting an object, check the following:
- Is the object's layer locked?
- Is the object locked?
- Are the edges hidden?
- Is the "Area select" box disabled (in General Preferences)?

If you keep selecting the wrong object, try again after you:
- Switch to Artwork mode.
- Zoom in.
- Hide the selected object; repeat if necessary.
- Lock the selected object; repeat if necessary.
- Choose View: Preview Selection (Option-⌘-Y) to preview *only* your selected object, so you know what you're about to lock, hide or edit.
- Put the object on top in another layer and hide that layer, or select Artwork for that layer.
- Use the Move command (Option-click on the Selection arrow in the Toolbox) to move selected objects (you can move them back later) a set distance.

Note: *See page 18 for more on hiding edges and zooming.*

Hide or lock all *except*...

To hide all *but* selected objects, choose Arrange: Hide with the Option key down (⌘-Option-3). To lock all *but* selected objects, choose Arrange: Lock with the Option key down (⌘-Option-1).

Digitizing a Logo
Making the Most of Illustrator's Template

Overview: *Scan a clean, enlarged version of your artwork; open the art as a template in Illustrator; analyze the curves of the template; trace the template; hide the template for final adjustments.*

1

Scanning a clean version of your artwork

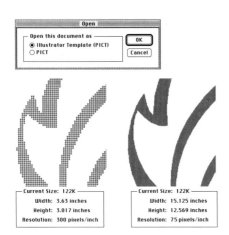

Two Illustrator templates with the same number of pixels but different pixel-per-inch ratios

Quick opening of templates

Hold down the Option key and choose File: New (⌘-Option-N) to directly open a template with a new file, bypassing the dialog box.

You can easily use Illustrator's Template layer to re-create traditional line art with the computer—easily, that is, if you know the tricks. Years after Rick Barry rendered the Breeders' Cup logo in black and white using traditional methods, he re-created it digitally in order to produce colorized versions. One version, using gradients, is shown above (for more about gradients, see *Chapter 5*).

1 Preparing a large, clean scan. Select a high-contrast image to re-create in Illustrator. Scan the image as black-and-white "line art" at 75 pixels per inch (ppi), but enlarged to 200–400 percent, and save it in PICT format. Most scanning software allows you to choose both the number of pixels (the actual resolution of the scan) as well as the pixel-per-inch viewing ratio. Normally, a 1" image scanned at 300 ppi will appear four times finer in detail than a 1" image scanned at 75 ppi. But when you open a PICT as an Illustrator template (choose File: Open and the dialog box at the left will appear), Illustrator won't display 300 ppi templates substantially better than 75 ppi templates. If, however, you scan at 400 percent and set the viewing ratio to 75 ppi, the enlarged image will appear crisp when opened as a template in Illustrator. Although the original logo was not very big, Barry had a stat produced at 12" wide and scanned it into the computer. Since his scanning software didn't permit adjusting the pixel-per-inch ratio, Barry used Photoshop to set the image to 75 ppi without changing the number of pixels before opening it as a template from Illustrator. **Note:** *Don't be concerned if you encounter 72 ppi (the resolution of your screen)—72 or 75 ppi is fine for templates.*

2 Adjusting the page size for the large template.
A large template will bleed over the edges of a standard paper size, so an easy way to make the template appear smaller while you work is to adjust Page Setup (from the File menu). Set the reduction to 25% and click OK.

3 Tracing the template. Look at the entire template and compare it to the original you have scanned. Are any of the curves or lines misrepresented in the template? Remember that the template is just a guide; if a discrepancy exists, follow the original. Working first in Artwork mode (from the View menu), use the Pen tool to trace your template (for help with the Pen tool, see page 4). Place the minimal number of points necessary to complete the object, and don't be too concerned with how closely you're matching the contour. Then, zoom in close (with the Zoom tool, marquee the area you wish to inspect) and use the Direct-selection tool to make adjustments to the length and angle of the direction lines until the Bézier curves properly fit the template.

4 Adjusting your views. As your image develops, view it in both Artwork and Preview modes, zoom in and out as necessary, and use the Hide / Show Template command (from the View menu, or ⌘-Shift-W) to control whether your template is hidden or visible.

5 Scaling the final. To place the finished illustration into another program, save the original, then choose Select All (⌘-A) and copy and paste the image into a new document. With the logo still selected, double-click the Scale tool to scale the final to meet your specific needs, making sure that you enable "Scale line weight." 🐎

2

The large template bleeding over the page

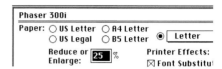

Adjusting Page Setup so the image fits within the page margins

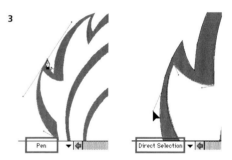

3

Using the Pen tool to draw curves and using the Direct-selection tool to adjust the curves (for info on Illustrator's cursors which change to reflect your action, see page 6)

4

Hiding the template to make final adjustments

Tracing a Scan

Using Custom Templates to Trace a Photo

STEUER

Overview: *Scan a photo; place it into its own layer in Illustrator; set layer options; trace the photo into the top layer with a color different from the scan; copy the finished illustration and paste it into a new document.*

Scan resolution for tracing

Bitmapped images saved in EPS format and placed into Illustrator display at approximately 75 pixels per inch (see page 80). Therefore, for maximum on-screen clarity, scan your image at two to three times the actual size at 75 ppi; you can then scale it down in Illustrator without losing detail. Since EPS images don't display more than 256 colors (8-bit), don't scan in more than 8-bit. Alternately, you can embed a TIFF as an image object; it displays at full resolution but increases the file size (see ⑥).

1

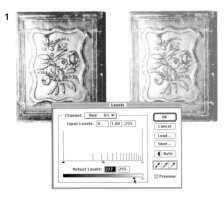

Original scan, then tinted in Photoshop

Illustrator's Template layer lets you trace over PICT images, which are displayed as two-tone, gray-and-white squares—making this template useless for low-contrast images. You can bypass the standard template by creating your own separate layer into which you can place a high-quality, continuous-tone image to use as a customized template. This image can be either a linked image or an embedded image object (for more on image input options, see pages 21–26 in *Chapter 1*, and ⑥).

For its mail-order catalogue, Exposures wanted to reproduce a leather relief daguerreotype case from the Smithsonian Institution's collection. With only a color snapshot to work with, Exposures commissioned me to produce the black-and-white line version they needed to create the molds for the new leather cover (artist's rendering shown above). Using Illustrator's layers functions, I traced over a linked EPS version of the scanned photo to re-create the original relief image as line art.

1 Scanning and tinting the photo. Scan the photo you wish to use as a tracing template. In a photo-manipulation program, tint your photo so it's a different color from the Illustrator path lines you'll be drawing with, and save it in EPS format. (If you can't tint a photo, temporarily trace with a colored line in Illustrator.) For the Exposures project, I optimized the low contrasts of the relief by scanning the photo in only 16 levels of gray

(4-bit). In Photoshop, I converted the image to "Indexed color" and, using Levels, tinted it red by increasing the output levels in the Red Channel.

2 **Making a new layer and placing the scan.** In Illustra-tor, open the Layers palette to see "Layer 1," in which you'll create your line illustration. Hold down the arrow in the Layers palette to access the pop-up menu to create a New Layer for your scan. Title the layer "Template," and enable your view and print options, but don't lock it. Click OK to apply these layer options. (To change them later, double-click on the layer title.) Then, select Place Art from the File menu to put the scan into your Template layer.

Making a new layer and placing the scan

3 **Reordering the layers.** Grab the Template layer and drag it below Layer 1 so the photo will be underneath your future line drawing. Now lock the template (click to remove the dot under the Pencil) and click on Layer 1 to make it the active layer for drawing.

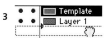

Moving the Template layer below Layer 1, then locking the template and activating Layer 1

4 **Tracing with geometric tools.** Examine your photo template. If you see objects that are almost symmetrical, use a Rectangle or an Oval tool to trace an approximation of that object, then use the transformation tools (Rotate, Scale, Reflect and Skew) to adjust the object to fit the photo better. Lastly, use the Direct-selection and Pen tools to reshape and redraw paths. For instance, I started the wavy borders surrounding the flowers with a rounded rec-tangle and used the Oval tool to approximate the circular flower pods. In both of these cases, I used transformation tools on the objects, redrew sections with the Pen tool, and used the Direct-selection tool to adjust the paths.

Using the Direct-selection tool to adjust paths drawn with the Oval and Pen tools

5 **Using the Pen and Brush tools to draw freeform objects.** For creating objects constructed of fluid lines and curves, use the Pen tool. When you are drawing squiggly or calligraphic marks, use the Brush tool. I used the Pen tool to create all flowers and leaves, and the Brush tool only for the squiggly centers of the flowers.

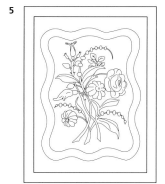

The final line illustration

Layering Colors

Coloring Black-and-White Images with Layers

Overview: *Create your black out-*
lines; set up layers in Illustrator for the
colors inside the lines and other layers
for background elements; place
black-and-white art into the
upper layer; color the image;
group outlines with their colors.

The background for the illustration, created in
the bottom two layers

An outline sketch

Choosing the "Transparent Whites" option when
saving in EPS format

While the most obvious way to trace placed images in
Illustrator is to put the image to be traced in a locked
lower layer and use an upper layer to trace the new Illustrator objects, in some cases you'll want your tracing
layer to be *below* a placed image. When illustrating a
three-ringed circus for a Ringling Brothers Barnum &
Bailey International Program, Michael Kline placed his
sketches with the whites transparent into a locked upper
layer so he could add color using Illustrator while maintaining a hand-sketched look.

1 Setting up your Illustrator layers. In Illustrator, create
enough layers for the various background elements in
your image. (For help making layers, see page 82.) Assign
each layer a different color to help keep track of which
objects will be in each layer (selected paths and anchor
points will be color-coded to match their layer). Then
create the background of your illustration in these layers.
When the background is ready, create at least two additional top layers for the figures you will be coloring.
For his circus illustration, Kline established four layers—
using the bottom layer ("Layer 4") to create the background itself and "Layer 3" to create the objects that
would be directly on top of the background.

2 Sketching or scanning a black-and-white drawing.
Scan a hand-drawn sketch or draw directly into a bit-mapped program. Save it as an EPS file, with a black-and-white preview (1-bit) and the "Transparent Whites" option. Kline drew figure sketches with a soft pencil on rough paper, scanned them, then saved them individually as transparent, 1-bit, black-and-white EPS files.

3 Placing your drawings into the top layer. From the Layers palette, make the top layer active (click on the layer name) and use the Place Art command (from the File menu) to place one of your drawings into the top layer. Then, lock the layer (remove the dot under the Pencil).

4 Coloring your drawings. You must tell Illustrator in which layer you will be drawing by activating and unlocking the second layer (there should be dots under the Eye and Pencil). Now, using filled colored objects without strokes, trace *under* your placed sketch. To view the color alone, hide the top layer.

5 Grouping your drawing with its colors. When you're finished coloring the first figure, select the placed EPS with the objects that colorize that figure and group them together. The colored, grouped figure will now be on the top layer, where you can easily reposition it within your composition.

3

The scanned drawing placed into Layer 1

4

The colorized drawing with the line drawing visible and the line drawing hidden

5

The drawing and the underlying color before and after being grouped together

---

Switching layers by selecting an object

If you are creating or editing objects with a number of layers unlocked, you don't have to use the Layers palette to switch your active layer. When you select an object from an unlocked layer, the layer that the selected object is on automatically becomes your new active layer. The next object you create will use the same paint style as the object you had selected and will be placed on that new active layer.

Moving the grouped, colorized figure around the composition

Multiple Layers

Creating a Poster from Multiple Sources

Overview: *Sketch and scan a composition; set up basic layers in Illustrator for the objects you will create; place art into temporary layers; trace the placed art; delete the temporary layers.*

1

Scanned photos of figures

Assembled collage and hand-traced sketch scanned

Scanned background photos

Multiple layers can be a lifesaver when you're constructing complex illustrations. Using these layers to isolate or combine specific elements will simplify your tasks substantially and save you an immense amount of production time. When The City Volunteer Corps (CVC) commissioned Nancy Stahl to design a New York City subway poster, she saved time and frustration by creating pairs of template-and-artwork layers for tracing and arranging various components of the poster.

1 Collecting and assembling source materials. Prepare your own source materials to use as tracing templates in Illustrator. For the CVC subway poster, Stahl took Polaroids of herself posed as each of the figures in the composition and scanned them into Adobe Photoshop, where she scaled them, and moved them into position. She then printed out the assembled "collage," roughly sketched in the other elements by hand and, with tracing paper, created a line version of the full composition to use as an overall template. She then scanned it into the computer.

Finally, Stahl scanned a number of photos showing different buildings in New York City's skyline for individual placement and tracing in Illustrator.

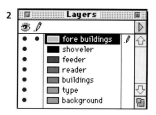

Setting up layers to isolate key elements

2 **Setting up illustration layers.** Before you begin to import any photos or drawings, take a few moments to set up layers to help you isolate the key elements in your illustration. (For help making layers, see page 82.) For the subway poster, before she actually started her Illustrator image, Stahl set up separate layers for the background, the type, and the buildings that would make up the skyline, as well as one layer for each of the figures and a final layer for the foreground buildings.

The temporary layer and choosing Place Art

3 **Placing art to use as templates.** You'll now need to create a few temporary layers for placing the artwork or scans you've collected to use as tracing templates. For each image you want to use as a template, make a new layer and use Place Art to select the scan or artwork to be placed into this layer. Then move the Template layer directly below the object layer upon which you will be tracing and lock it. Stahl created a layer, which she named "EPS Images," and then placed the buildings that she would be tracing for the skyline. Using the Layers palette, she then moved this new skyscraper template below her "buildings" layer, onto which she created the Illustrator buildings, and then locked the EPS Images layer.

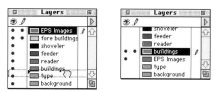

Moving the layer and setting up the write and view options for tracing

4 **Drawing into your layers.** Now you can begin drawing and tracing elements into your compositional layers. Activate the layer in which you want to draw (click on the layer's name), unlock and view the layer (there should be dots in the Eye and Pencil columns) and start to work. Use the Layers palette to lock, unlock or hide layers, as well as to toggle between Preview and Artwork modes (Option-click on the Pencil dot), switch your active layer or add a new layer. By so maneuvering, Stahl could easily trace a group of skyscrapers, create type against a locked background or develop one figure at a time.

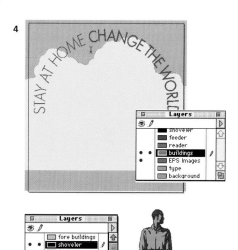

Isolating elements by viewing and unlocking only the essential layers

5

Clicking on a visible and unlocked layer to make it active for placing new art

6

Moving placed art within a layer to trace different objects

7

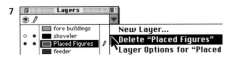

Using the Delete option from the Layers palette pop-up menu

Changing placed art

Select the EPS you wish to replace, and choose Place Art from the Edit menu. Choose your new art, in the dialog box which then appears, click to Replace the selected EPS with this new one. If you didn't intend to replace an EPS, click Ignore (which places the new EPS *in addition* to the one that was selected), or just Cancel.

---

5 Adding new placed art to a lower layer. If you need to import art into an existing layer, you must first make the layer visible and unlocked (in the Layers palette, you should see dots in the Eye and Pencil columns) and then make it the active layer. For the subway poster, when Stahl needed additional building references, she viewed and unlocked EPS Images, clicked on it to make it the active layer and then used the Place Art command.

6 Moving placed art within a layer. Stahl's reference photos showed New York's buildings clustered differently from the way she wanted them for her illustration, so she devised a way to space the buildings as she worked. After tracing over one building, she unlocked EPS Images, moved the cluster of buildings slightly and relocked the layer. She then traced a different skyscraper in the new location and repeated the procedure for each building.

7 Deleting layers when you finish using them. Extra layers with placed art can take up quite a bit of disk space, so when you finish using a template, first save the file. Then, from the Layers palette, click on the layer you are ready to remove and choose the Delete option from the Layers palette pop-up menu. Finally, use Save As to save this new version of the illustration with a meaningful new name and version number (such as "CVC without EPS-3.0"). Stahl eventually deleted all the layers she created as templates so she could save her final poster with all the illustration layers but none of the templates or placed pictures. 💿

Moving an object from one layer to another

To move a selected object to another layer: open the Layers palette, grab the colored dot to the right of the object's layer and drag it to the desired layer. To move a copy of an object: hold down the Option key while you drag.

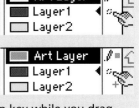

STAHL

Gallery: Nancy Stahl

Working with the computer, artists can now miraculously breathe new life into finished works. Nancy Stahl had created this image from one of her handpainted illustrations using Illustrator 3.2 (before there were layers). In order to simplify reworking this image, Stahl began by using Illustrator 5.5 to separate elements into distinct layers: the background, a layer for each of the figures, and a few layers to isolate the various foreground elements. She moved objects to the correct layers by dragging the colored dots representing them in the Layers palette. (See Tip at left, and reworked image on page 186.)

Viewing Details

Using Layers and Views for Organization

Overview: *Establish your working layers; use layers to organize distinct categories of elements; save zoom levels and viewpoints using the New View command.*

General organizational layers

Additional layers created to isolate categories of elements

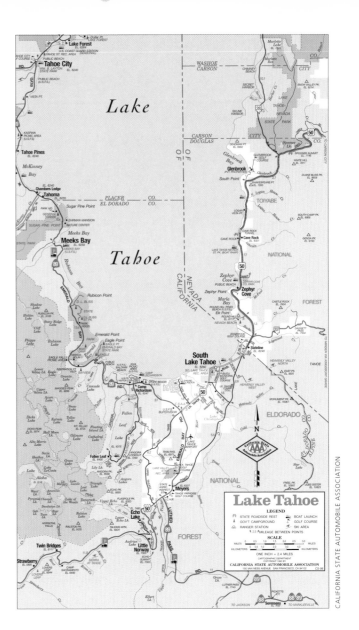

In addition to providing an ideal method for overlapping compositional elements, layers can help organize complex illustrations, even when many of the elements appear to exist on the same visual plane. When the California State Automobile Association (CSAA) creates road maps using Illustrator, the cartography department uses layers to delineate the different categories of labeling information. Even on the fastest computers, however, you can waste a lot of time zooming in and out, hiding and showing layers and toggling various layers between Preview and Artwork modes. That's why the CSAA saves frequently used views to navigate quickly and easily around its large format maps.

1 Creating organizational layers. In addition to layers you create for compositional elements (such as background or figures), try creating separate layers for each category of labeling information you're including. If you construct your image with layers organized by the category of element, it becomes very simple to view and change all similar text or objects at once. For its Lake Tahoe map, the CSAA created individual layers for park lands, creeks, lakes and boundary lines, as well as layers for roads, type, symbols and the legend.

2 Saving frequently used views. Instead of wasting precious time zooming in and out of your image and scrolling around to find a specific detail, you can preserve your current viewpoint for immediate return at another time. Along with "remembering" the specific section you zoomed to, saved views remember which of your layers were in Preview or Artwork modes. To save your current view, simply choose View: New View, name your current view and click OK. Your view will then be added to the bottom of the View menu. Each successive view you save will appear at the bottom of the menu. The CSAA saved separate views for each area of the map requiring repeated attention, which included each of the four corners, the legend box and three additional locations.

3 Using views. To recall a saved view, choose the desired view from the list at the bottom of the View menu. Using Edit Views, you can rename or delete views, although you cannot, unfortunately, change the viewpoints themselves. Another glitch is that Edit Views lists the most recently created or renamed view last, not alphabetically, so getting your layers to list in a specific order takes a bit of organization. 🌀

Saving and naming a viewpoint using New View

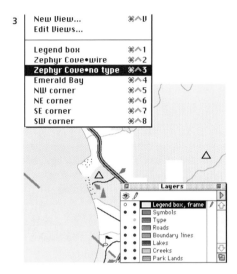

Recalling a view, which resets the zoom level, what portion of the image is visible, and which layers are visible or hidden, locked or unlocked

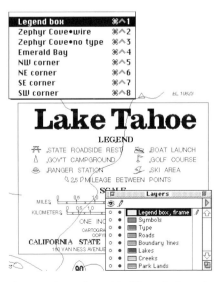

The Legend Box View, with all layers in Artwork

Layer Registration

Paste Remembers Layers' Magic Alignment

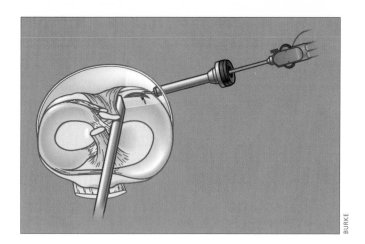

BURKE

Overview: *Create enough layers for all stages of your sequence; use New View to save settings for which layers are visible for each stage; control which layers print for proofing; set "Paste remembers layers" for separating stages for final printing.*

1

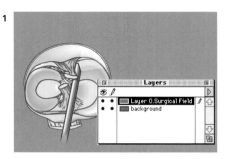

The background layer (the filled rectangle only) and main surgical layer, "Layer 0"

2

Selecting saved views to recall various stages

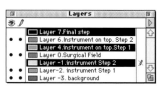

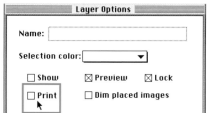

Shift-selecting multiple layers and double-click-ing to disable the Print option in Layer Options

Organizing a series of interrelated illustrations in perfect registration with each other is simple using layers. This medical illustration shows three of the nine stages in a series that Christopher Burke created for Linvatec Corporation demonstrating the surgical procedure for repairing a knee injury once the fiber-optic light/camera is in place to illuminate the injury site.

1 Creating layers to illustrate the unifying aspects of the series. Create the necessary layers into which you'll construct basic elements common to the whole series of illustrations (for help making layers, see page 82). Burke's basic layers for this surgical technique illustration were the surgical layer illustrating the knee, and the background.

2 Simplifying the creation, viewing and proofing of the various stages of your illustration. Once the unifying aspects of your illustration are in place, use additional layers for creating variants. Use the Layers palette to hide and show various layers and thus isolate each of the different versions. Burke created all stages for the su-turing technique in the same document. As he created a layer for a specific stage of the procedure, he would in-clude that stage number in the layer name. For the num-bering system, Burke named the main surgical layer "Layer 0"—this layer would appear in every stage. He numbered each progressive layer above it "1, 2, 3…" and then used "–1, –2, –3…" for each subsequent layer below.

When using layers to create a series of related illustrations, use the New View command to help you keep track of which layers need to be visible or hidden for each individual illustration. Once you've done this, choose New View from the View menu and save these settings. By selecting the proper view for each illustration from the bottom of the View menu, you'll easily be able to toggle between each stage in the series.

To avoid having to make unnecessary changes to multiple documents, keep the file together as long as you can. Therefore, the safest way to print proofs of your separate illustrations from this one large file is to use Layer Options to determine which layers will print for each version. Hold down your Shift key to select the layers you're choosing *not* to print, double-click on one of these selected layers to open Layer Options and disable the Print option to prevent these layers from printing.

3 Preparing final versions for printing. In General Preferences, enable "Paste remembers layers" to ensure that your objects will stay in the correct layers, and that layers will be automatically replicated as you move objects to other files. With this option enabled (I always keep it enabled) use the colored dots in the Layers palette to move and copy objects to other layers (see Tip on page 88).

To print the final illustrations, copy each completed stage into its own file. Select your saved views for the first stage, making sure all the layers necessary to the illustration are visible and unlocked (there should be dots under the Pencil and the Eye). If you've hidden or locked any elements individually, choose Unlock All (⌘-2) and Show All (⌘-4) from the Arrange menu. Then select and copy this version, and, in a new document, use Paste In Front (⌘-F). When you use Paste In Front, all needed layers will miraculously appear in the Layers palette and the image will be in perfect registration so you can still move objects back and forth between files. Repeat this step for each stage of the illustration. ☙

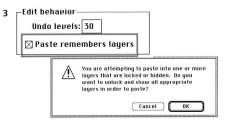

Setting "Paste remembers layers" in Preferences and the warning you'll get if you try to paste an object copied from a locked or hidden layer (see page 88 for moving objects to other layers)

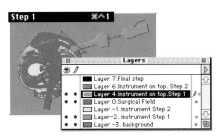

Choosing Step1 view, then selecting all needed layers for copying and pasting into a new file

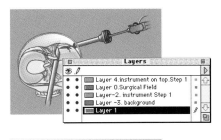

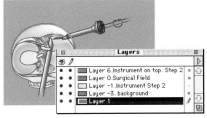

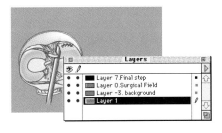

Each of the three stages pasted into its own document, with layers appearing automatically

BARNEY (Illustrator), FRANSON (designer) / BARNEY MCKAY DESIGN

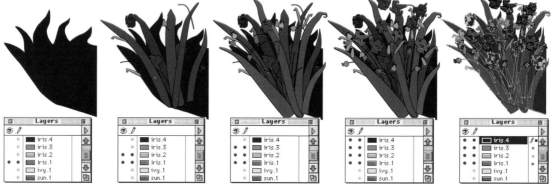

Gallery: Jeffrey Barney / Barney McKay Design

For this image, serving as part of a five-tier pop-up promotion for The
Secret Garden, *Jeffrey Barney used dozens of layers to isolate various elements. Barney began by creating seven separate documents which, from
front to back, were Ivy, Poppies, Roses, Irises, Mary (the girl), Sunflowers
and Tree/Sky—each of the files containing between four and seven
named layers. To arrange elements into the final five files for the pop-up
properly, Barney kept the "Paste remembers layers" option enabled (see
page 92). In this way, he could move objects between files while keeping
them on the correct layers and in perfect registration. He needed other
arrangements of different layers for other materials, including the close-
ups of Irises and Sunflowers for a CD cover (shown with an "onionskin"
overlay) and other print materials designed with Scott Franson.*

Gallery: Dorothea Taylor-Palmer

For this image, artist Dorothea Taylor-Palmer used the technique of placing one of her drawings on a top layer and painting the colored swatches in layers below (see page 82). She began with a traditional sketch and experimented with running it through a copier while moving it slightly until she captured the illusion of movement she had in mind. After scanning the sketch into a bitmapped program, Taylor-Palmer saved it as a transparent, 1-bit EPS file, which she then placed into Illustrator. After locking the layer with the sketch, she created another layer and moved it below the sketch. Into the lower layer, Taylor-Palmer painted swaths of color to show through the white portions of the placed sketch.

TAYLOR-PALMER

PALMER

Gallery: Charly Palmer

Although a professional illustrator for many years, Charly Palmer has only recently begun using Illustrator, under the tutelage of his wife, Dorothea Taylor-Palmer. Even though his method of working is fairly similar to that which Taylor-Palmer used for the image above, his own vision and hand are strongly evident in this profile. After placing a scanned drawing that was saved as a transparent EPS onto an upper layer and locking it, Palmer used colors and blends to complete the composition.

Varied Perspective

Analyzing Different Views of Perspective

Advanced Technique

Overview: *Draw and scan a sketch; establish working layers using your sketch as a template; in a "Guides" layer, draw a series of lines to establish perspective; make the perspective lines into guides; using layers to control what is visible, construct your image according to the applicable perspective guides.*

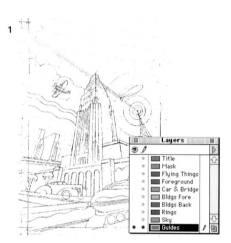

1

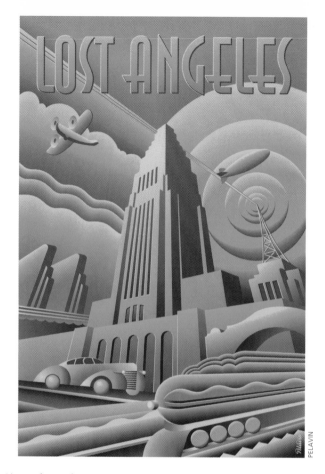

PELAVIN

The template with a custom layer ready for placement of guides

2

Dragging a perspective line to form a "V," then blending to create in-between perspective lines

Since the Italian Renaissance, the conventions of vanishing-point perspective have helped artists to organize their two-dimensional artwork. You can use Adobe Illustrator to establish vanishing points with the help of object guides. The following few pages include perspective approaches by two different artists. This section will not so much teach you how to construct an image using vanishing points as it will help you to translate your knowledge of perspective into techniques to use within Illustrator. The slightly distorted perspective in Danny Pelavin's "Lost Angeles" demonstrates how that knowledge can translate into results that are quite fantastic.

1 With a scanned sketch as a template, setting up the necessary layers. Draw a sketch of your composition establishing some basic perspective guidelines. Scan the sketch, save it in PICT format and open it as a template in Illustrator. Once in Illustrator, create the essential number of layers to isolate the various compositional elements, plus one extra layer for your guides.

2 Establishing the location of vanishing points. Activate your "Guides" layer (by clicking on the layer name) and lock all other layers. Using your template as a reference, decide where to place the first vanishing point and use the Pen tool to draw a line along the horizon line through the vanishing point. (It is fine if your vanishing point extends beyond the picture border.) With the Direct-selection tool, select the anchor point from the end of the line that is opposite the vanishing point. Grab the point, then hold down your Option key and swing this copy of the line up so it encompasses the uppermost object that will be constructed along the vanishing point. You should now have a "V" that goes from your horizon line, through your vanishing point, then to an upper portion of your composition. To create in-between lines through the same vanishing point, select both of the original lines, use the Blend tool to click first on the outer anchor point of one of the lines, then on the outer anchor point of the other line, and next specify the number of in-between steps. For each different vanishing point, repeat the above procedure. While creating his perspective guides in Illustrator, Pelavin discovered that his previous technique of using a thumbtack and a piece of string was nowhere near as accurate.

3 Making your perspective lines into guides. Once you have completed your perspective lines, choose Select All (⌘-A, or Edit: Select All), then choose Object: Guides: Make (⌘-5). You have now transformed the lines into nonprinting dashed guides. In addition to being able to lock or hide your guides from within the Layers palette, you can take advantage of some unique properties. If you wish to select, align, or manipulate your guides, then disable the Object: Guides: Lock option (by selecting it).

3

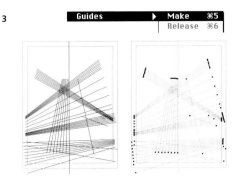

Perspective lines before and after being made into guides

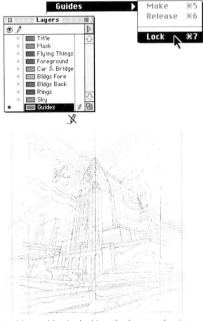

Locking guides by locking the layer and using the Lock/Unlock toggle from Object: Guides

Grouping guides with objects

When guides are unlocked, you can select them freely as objects. This option applies to horizontal guides dragged from the ruler as well as custom guides. Try grouping guides with related objects so you can move, hide, scale and rotate them along with their associated objects.

4 Hide Template ⌘⇧W
Hide Rulers ⌘R
Hide Page Tiling
Hide Edges ⌘⇧H
Hide Guides

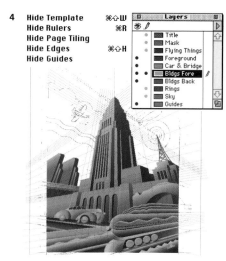

Tools for hiding and showing elements

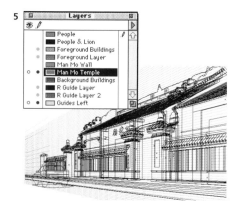

"Guides Left" layer shown with buildings drawn in Artwork mode on Man Mo Temple layer

TATE

Tate's final image

Note, however, that the Lock/Unlock Guides option will affect all open documents. If you wish to transform your guides back into objects, unlock them, select the guides you wish to convert, and choose Objects: Guides: Release from the Object menu.

4 Creating your illustration using guides and templates as necessary. As you actually create your illustration, control what you're viewing on the screen at any one time with the Hide/Show menu. Also, from the Layers palette, toggle to control which layers are visible, hidden, locked, unlocked, or in Preview or Artwork mode.

5 Variations on a theme. Pelavin's solution to perspective guides on the Mac is a reflection of his drawing style. Other artists use the same techniques differently. For his "Man Mo Temple," instead of reserving one layer for perspective guides, Clark Tate used three separate layers. Because of the nature of the architectural detailing he was creating, Tate wanted more than just general perspective lines; he wanted to be able to actually create every building line from his perspective grid. Since having so many lines is visually distracting, Tate created two layers for his right-facing perspectives, each containing every other line, with a third layer reserved for the left-facing perspective. With this system, Tate could use the Layers palette to show only the specific perspective lines he required for the construction of each object.

Scanning true horizontals and verticals for tracing

When preparing templates for detailed renderings that rely on true horizontal and vertical lines (such as the architectural images in this technique or the Andrea Kelley computer renderings on pages 114 and 158), you must scan your template image into the computer perfectly straight. Take an image (or copy of an image) and cut the edge of the paper perfectly square to the image so you can line up the paper edge to the edge of the scanner bed itself. —*Tip by Andrea Kelley*

Blends & Gradients

5

Blends & Gradients

Introduction...

Keeping blends grouped...

Illustrator automatically groups blended objects together.

- The two objects that initiate the blend won't be part of the group, however, so you should either group these objects with the blend or delete them.

- As long as you don't ungroup a blend, you can easily reselect it by clicking twice with the Group-selection tool on any object within a blend.

- Use the Direct-selection tool to adjust objects within a blend.

About the Gradient palette...

To open your Gradient palette, double-click on the Gradient tool or on a gradient name in the Paint Style palette, or choose Window: Show Gradient.

- Click on the lower edge of a gradient to add a new color.

- Hold down your Option key to drag a copy of a color pointer.

- With the Eyedropper tool, Control-click in your image to load that color into a pointer.

- Drag one pointer over another to swap their colors.

What is the difference between a blend and a gradient?

Think of blends as a way to "morph" one object or color, or shape and color, to another. After selecting two objects, click with the Blend tool *exactly* on corresponding anchor points on each object and specify the number of steps you want to place in between. Using fewer steps results in clearly distinguishable objects, while a larger number of steps results in an almost "airbrushed" effect.

When the blend first appears, it will be selected and grouped. If you Undo immediately (⌘-Z), the blend will be deleted, and your two source objects will be selected, ready for you to blend again. If you later wish to change your blend after completing it, you must select the blend only (try clicking twice with Group-selection tool), delete the blend, select your two source objects and blend again.

Gradients are purely color transitions, which you can select as a Fill style by clicking on the Gradient icon on the right side of the Paint Style palette. You can fill objects with gradients that are either radial (circular from the center) or linear (in straight lines). Make your own gradients by placing and spacing pointers representing colors along the lower edge of the color scale in the Gradient palette, or by adjusting the midpoint of the color transition as a result of sliding the diamond shapes along the top of the scale. Illustrator saves gradients by name, so changing the colors or styling of a previously used gradient will automatically update all objects filled with that gradient. You can adjust the length, direction and center-point location of selected gradients, as well as unify blends across multiple objects by clicking and dragging with the Gradient-fill tool (page 108). To fill type with gradients, convert the type to an object (see page 138). To create the illusion of a gradient within a stroke, convert the stroke to a filled object (see Tip on page 64).

New in Illustrator 6, you can use Object: Expand to convert gradients into blends (see ⑥).

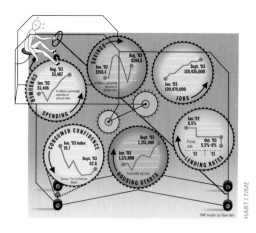

Gallery: Steve Hart / *Time*

Gradients make shifts of color very simple; Steve Hart first designed a gradient for one gear, then only needed to duplicate the gradient and change the color for each of the other gears.

Gallery: Kurt Hess / Agnew Moyer Smith, Inc.

Blends are necessary for creating realistic, irregularly shaped reflections of light (see page 112 for help with realistic blends).

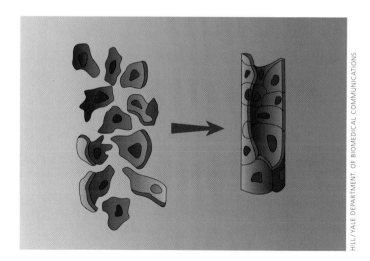

Gallery: Wendolyn Hill / Yale Department of Biomedical Communications

Using the Gradient tool, Wendolyn Hill changed the direction of the gradient to create the illusion of inside versus outside in this medical illustration of "vasculogenesis," or vessel formation.

Examining Blends

Learning When to Use Gradients or Blends

Overview: *Examine your objects; for linear or circular fills, create basic gradients; for contouring fills into complex objects, create blends.*

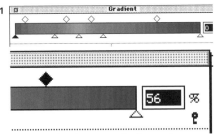

Adjusting the placement of colors, and rate of color transition in the Gradient palette

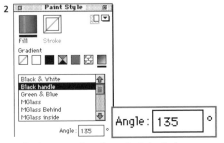

Selecting a gradient from the Paint Style palette and setting the gradient Angle

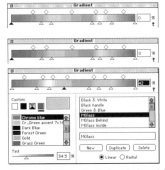

One gradient duplicated and altered for application to different related objects

You need to take a number of factors into consideration when you're deciding whether to create color transitions with blends or gradients. *Can* the object be created with either is the first question, and Steve Hart's magnifying glass, created for *Time* magazine, is a clear-cut example of when to use gradients or blends.

1 Designing gradients. Choose an object you'd like to fill with a linear gradient. Open the Gradient palette (double-click on the Gradient tool), click New and type a name. This initially minimal gradient has two colors: white (at the left) and black (at the right). Click on the left pointer to display its position on the scale from 0–100% (in this case 0%). Slide the pointer to the right to increase the percentage displayed in the scale, and increase the black area of the gradient. Click on the bottom edge of the scale to add additional pointers. Click on a pointer to access its numeric position, or to change its color or tint. Between every two pointers is a diamond shape indicating the midpoint of the color transition (from 0–100% between each color pair). Grab and drag a diamond to adjust the color transition rate, or type a new position into the percent field.

2 Filling objects with gradients and making adjustments. To fill your object with a gradient, select the object, click on the Gradient icon (on the right side of the Paint Style palette) and choose your gradient from the list. Once you've filled the object you can continue to experiment with the gradient by adjusting the spacing of the pointers and diamonds and by setting the angle of the gradient in the Paint Style palette. To create colored gradients, either use one of the custom colors mixed with its own tints (see page 62) or use process colors. Hart filled his magnifying glass handle with a gradient at a 135° angle. He used the Duplicate command in the Gradient palette to create slightly different variants for gradients representing the metal rings around the outside, along the inside, and inside behind the glass.

3 Using blends for irregular or contoured transitions.
For domed, kidney-shaped or contoured objects (such as shadows), only a blend will do. Make two objects with the same number of points (try scaling one to create the other). Set each to the desired color and click on a related anchor point on one, then the other, with the Blend tool. Try setting the number of steps that the Blend dialog box recommends (you can experiment with fewer, but there is rarely a need for more). The more similar the colors, the fewer steps you'll need. (See the Adobe CD's "Smooth blends" for technical specifications for calculating smooth blends.) Hart used blends for only the glow in the glass (20 steps), the knob of the handle (22 steps) and the shadow (12 steps). 🫛

Automatically updating colors

For Gradients:
- If you use custom colors for your gradients, changes to your custom color will automatically update whatever gradients use that color.

For Blends:
- If you blend between two objects that are tints of the same custom color (Hint: Tints of 0% = White), then changes to the custom color will also update the blend! —*Tip by Agnew Moyer Smith, Inc.*

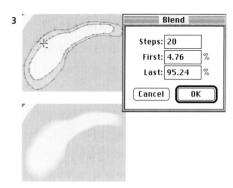

3

Clicking first on a selected point of one path, then on a selected point of the other to open the dialog box to specify 20 steps; and the blended objects

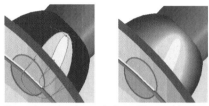

Two selected paths, and after a 22-step blend

Before and after a 12-step blend to create a shadow

The final image as it appeared in Time

Shades of Blends

Creating Architectural Linear Shading

Overview: *Create an architectural form using rectangles; copy and paste one rectangle in front; delete the top and bottom paths and blend between the two sides.*

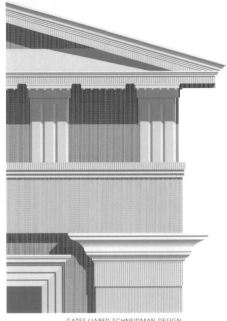

GATES / JARED SCHNEIDMAN DESIGN

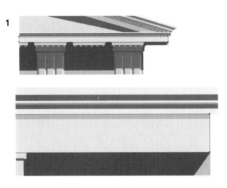

A selected rectangle copied and pasted in front in full view, and in close-up

The top and bottom deleted with the sides selected

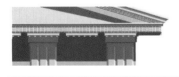

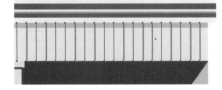

The full blend and a close-up detail (Shift-⌘-H hides selection edges, see page 19)

Without much difficulty, Illustrator can help simulate the traditional artistic conventions for rendering architectural details. Jared Schneidman Design developed a simple but exacting method to apply vertical line shading.

1 Creating an architectural structure. After establishing the overall form, color and tonality of your illustration, select and copy one rectangle. Choose ⌘-F (Edit: Paste In Front) to place the copy on top, then set the fill to None and the stroke to .1-pt Black. Choose Window: Show Info to note the line's width in points. (Use ⌘-Control-U to toggle between inches, millimeters and points.) Calculate the width of the rectangle divided by the spacing you'd like between lines. Subtract 2 (for the sides you have) to find the proper number of steps for this blend.

2 Deleting the top and bottom and blending the sides. Deselect the copy, Shift-Direct-select the top and bottom paths and delete, leaving the sides selected. With the Blend tool, click on the top point of each side and specify the number of steps you determined above. 🍃

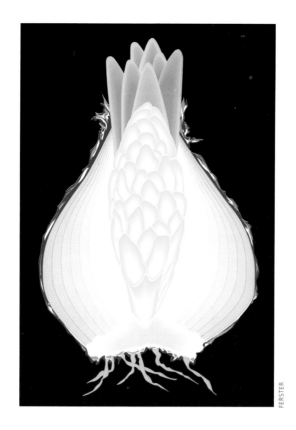

Gallery: Gary Ferster

For his client Langeveld Bulb, Gary Ferster used blends to create the in-between layers in this flower bulb. He began by styling the outer peel with a .5-pt stroke in a dark brown custom color and filled the object with a lighter brown custom color. He then created the inner layer, filled it white, and gave it a .5-pt white stroke. Selecting both objects, Ferster specified a six-step blend that simultaneously "morphed" each progressive layer into the next while lightening the layers towards white. Blends were also used to create the leafy greens, yellow innards and all the other soft transitions between colors.

Popular San Francisco Buildings

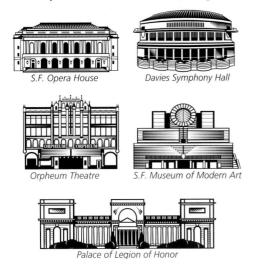

S.F. Opera House

Davies Symphony Hall

Orpheum Theatre

S.F. Museum of Modern Art

Palace of Legion of Honor

Fish in the San Francisco Bay

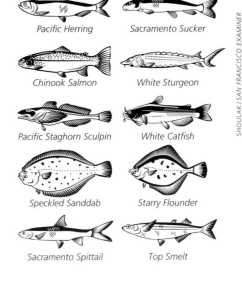

Pacific Herring

Sacramento Sucker

Chinook Salmon

White Sturgeon

Pacific Staghorn Sculpin

White Catfish

Speckled Sanddab

Starry Flounder

Sacramento Spittail

Top Smelt

SHOULAK / SAN FRANCISCO EXAMINER

San Francisco Museum of Modern Art

Bluegill

Gallery: Joe Shoulak / *San Francisco Examiner*

Joe Shoulak frequently uses blends to create in-between repetitive shapes. Given the deadlines at a busy newspaper, the Blend tool has proved an essential production tool for generating the horizontal and vertical lines in buildings (for an article on "Retrofitting the Arts") as well as the sequence of organic shapes (as in the fins of fish for the series "Bay in Peril"). Shoulak also relies heavily on filters—using the Offset Path filter to create white inset shapes that follow the contours of outlines, and the Outline Path filter to convert all stroked lines in final images to filled objects (so he doesn't accidentally resize without properly scaling the line weight). See Chapter 6 for more on filters.

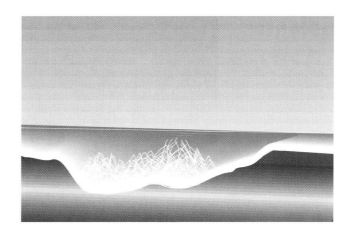

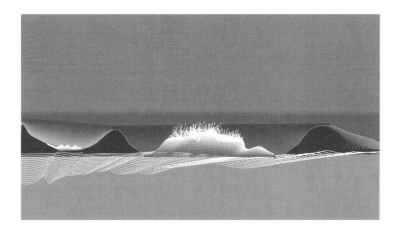

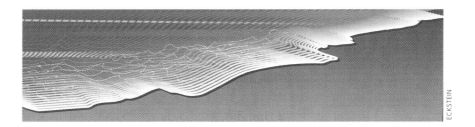

ECKSTEIN

Gallery: Linda Eckstein

Linda Eckstein created these beautiful seascapes in Illustrator using blends. Instead of merely controlling the regularity of blends to depict the ocean, Eckstein needed to control the irregularity of the blends as well. On the back layer of her image are blends that establish both the general composition and the broad color schemes. On top of these tonal-filled, object blends are irregularly shaped linear blends that form the waves and surf. Using the Direct-selection tool, she isolated individual points and groups of points to stretch and distort the waves.

Unified Gradients

Redirecting Fills with the Gradient Tool

Overview: *Fill objects with gradients; use the Gradient-fill tool to adjust the length and direction of fills and locations of centers across multiple objects.*

Fill

Clicking and dragging with the Gradient tool to establish the gradient's rate and direction

Before and after setting the direction of the radial fills to unify shapes and create volume

How long can a gradient be?

Click and drag with the Gradient tool anywhere in your image window; you don't need to stay within the objects themselves. Also, see the *Wow!* disk for Eve Elberg's "Comet" Gradient tool exercise.

STEUER

When you first create gradients, they won't necessarily look the way you want them to. The Gradient-fill tool allows you to stretch gradients across multiple objects by applying one unifying length and direction to the entire group. I created this image, titled "Finesse" (as a memorial to my grandmother, a master bridge player), for a review of Illustrator in *Computer Artist* magazine. In the crown especially, I went crazy with the Gradient tool.

1 **Filling objects with the same gradient.** Select a number of objects to fill as a unit and click on a gradient fill in the Paint Style palette to fill each object with that gradient. Keep your objects selected.

2 **Unifying gradients with the Gradient tool.** With the Gradient tool from the Toolbox, click and drag from the point where you want the gradient to begin to the point where you want it to end. Hold down the Shift key if you want to constrain the angle of the gradient. To relocate a radial gradient's center, click with the Gradient tool. Experiment until you get the desired effect. Repeat selecting, filling and making use of the Gradient tool to unify the gradients for other groups of objects. 🌰

GORSKA

Gallery: Caryl Gorska

Caryl Gorska created "Bountiful Harvest" as a package design for Nunes Farms' dried fruits, nuts and chocolates. She used the Gradient-fill tool to customize her radial blends (made of process colors). Parchment paper, scanned in Photoshop and saved in EPS, is the background layer (see Chapter 4).

Resetting gradients to the default settings

After you make adjustments with the Gradient-fill tool, other objects that you fill with gradients will have the same altered angles. To "re-zero" gradients, view the right side of the Paint Style palette, click on the Custom Color icon and choose a color. When you next choose a gradient, angles will have the default setting. Or, for linear gradients, you can type "0" in the Angle field.

Gallery: Kerry Gavin

Kerry Gavin is the first to admit that without the Gradient tool, he couldn't have created the image "Golden Parachutes." The miniature version of "Parachutes" at the right shows the figure in the room without the benefit of the Gradient tool. The sense of place and light that is so present in Gavin's final version is noticeably absent in the miniature, where the fills aren't customized.

Gallery: Hugh Whyte / Lehner & Whyte

In this image designed for a spring calendar, Hugh Whyte used gradients and the Gradient tool to create a colorful, cut-out look that is both flat and volumetric. The Artwork view at the right reveals that Whyte constructed the image entirely of gradients, with no blends.

Unlocking Realism

Creating Metallic Reflections with Blends

Overview: *Form the basic shapes of objects; create tonal boundaries for future blends that follow the contours of the objects; copy, scale, recolor and adjust the anchor points of tonal boundaries; blend highlights and shadows.*

1

Designing the basic objects and choosing a base tone (Note: Gray strokes added to distinguish objects)

Creating tonal boundaries for future blends by following the contours of the objects

Achieving photorealism with Illustrator may appear prohibitively complex and intimidating, but with a few simple rules-of-thumb, some careful planning and the eye of an artist, it can be done. Brad Neal, of Thomas•Bradley Illustration & Design, demonstrates with this image that you don't need an airbrush to achieve metallic reflectivity, specular highlights or warm shadows.

1 Preparing a detailed sketch that incorporates a strong light source, and setting up your palette.
Before you actually start your illustration, create a sketch that establishes the direction of your light source. Then, in Illustrator, set up your color palette (see *Chapter 3*). Choose one color as a "base tone," the initial tint from which all blends will be built, and fill the entire object with that value. After you create the basic outlines of your illustration, work in Artwork mode to create separate paths—following the contours of your objects—for each of your major color transitions. After completing the initial line drawing of the lock set, Neal visually and then physically "mapped" out the areas that would contain the

shading. He added a few highlights and reflections in the later stages of the project, but the majority of blends were mapped out in advance.

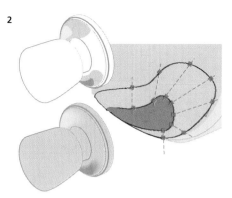

2 Using your color transition paths to create blends.

Next, use the contouring paths you've created to map out your tonal boundaries. Choose one of the objects and fill it with the same color and tonal value as its underlying shape. In the Neal locks, this initial color is always the same color and value selected for the base color. Then, copy the object and use ⌘-F to Paste In Front. Next, fill this copy with a highlight or shadow value, scale it down and manipulate it into the correct position to form the highlight or shadow area. You can accomplish this step by one of two methods: by scaling the object using the Scale tool or by selecting and pulling in individual anchor points with the Direct-selection tool. In order to ensure smooth blends without ripples or irregular transitions, the anchor points of the inner and outer objects must be as closely aligned as possible and must contain the same number of points; *this is a critical stage of the process.*

Finally, to complete this highlight or shadow, select both objects and, with the Blend tool, click on a selected anchor point of one object, next on the corresponding anchor point of the other object, then specify the minimal size blend to achieve a smooth look. The blend in Figure 2 required eight in-between steps.

Pasting In Front a scaled down and adjusted copy with the same number of aligned points

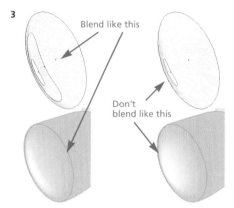

Adding an in-between contour to help control the rate and shape of blends; blending with too few contours flattens the image

3 Blending in smaller increments.
Some blend situations may require more than two objects to achieve the desired look. For instance, to control the rate at which the tone changes or the way an object transforms throughout the blended area, you may wish to add an intermediate object and blend in two stages, instead of one.

4 Using blends to soften hard transitions.
Always use blends when making tonal transitions, even when you need a stark contrast shadow or highlight. A close look at Neal's shadow reveals a very short but distinct blend.

Long, close-up and Artwork close-up views of highlight and shadow transitions

Blending Realism

Keeping Blends Clean and Accessible

Overview: *Delete the side of a rectangle; offset the top and bottom open ends horizontally; blend this open object with another smaller, darker object; place caps on top and bottom; create contouring blends on the sides.*

The final illustration in Artwork mode

Two copies of a rectangle pasted on top with right side removed and points shifted left

Before and after blending offset objects

A quick look at an illustration in Artwork mode usually reveals a lot about how an image is constructed. However, when you look at Andrea Kelley's Apple Computer product illustrations in Artwork mode, you would probably mistakenly guess that she uses gradients to create her tonal changes. But since her renderings are used on-screen as well as printed, Kelley often uses blends for more exacting control over her tones (gradients can look banded on the screen even if they print well). Her techniques can help you create a monitor screen with a soft, ambient lighting effect.

1 Creating an "offset" blend. Make a rectangle and fill it with a 35% tint of black. Copy and hide (⌘-3) the rectangle, then use Paste In Front (⌘-F) to place the copy on top. With the Direct-selection tool, select and delete the right side of the path. Since open objects still remain filled in Illustrator, the object looks identical in Preview mode. With the Direct-selection tool, grab the top right point and slide it to the left slightly (about .25"), using the Shift key to constrain movement horizontally. Then grab the lower right point and slide it over to the halfway point on the rectangle, (again, use your Shift key). Now select and copy the adjusted object, use Paste In Front to move the copy and change the tint of this new object to 65%. Use the same technique you did before, but this time slide the bottom right point all the way to the left and the top right point over towards the left corner. (This polygon should look almost like a triangle.) Next, select the top right points of the two objects you just made, click on each point with the Blend tool and use the recommended number of steps. In Artwork mode, instead of the expected sea of diagonally blended lines running across the screen, your monitor should appear "clean" and uncomplicated.

2 **Creating the rounded top and bottom.** Show (⌘-4) your hidden back rectangle. With the Pen tool, draw a bow-shaped "cap" filled with a 35% tint of black that overlaps the top of your blend with a long, almost horizontal curve. Have the points meet beyond the blend on either side, arcing into a bow shape above. To add a touch of shadow detail, copy the bottom path of the bow (the long, almost horizontal line) and use Paste In Front to place a copy of the path. Change the Fill style of this path to None, with a .25-pt stroke weight at a 40% tint of black. Lastly, copy and reflect the full filled cap along the horizontal axis, place it along the bottom of the blended monitor screen and set it to a 10% tint of black.

3 **Contouring the sides.** To create the illusion that the monitor is inset, create three long, overlapping rectangles on the left edge of your blended monitor screen, running from cap to cap. (Adjust the points as necessary so the objects run flush against the cap.) From left to right, make the rectangles 10%, 50% and 45% tints of black. Select the right two rectangles and blend between them, then lock the blend so you can easily blend the left two rectangles. Repeat from the right side of the monitor with rectangles of 5%, 10% and 25% (from left to right). You can make the monitor case the same way as the screen, but shade the case with 10% on the left, blending to 25% on the right. (See *Chapter 8*'s Advanced Techniques for blending and masking curved objects.) 💿

2

Rounded "caps" put on top and bottom of the blended screen

3

Placing three rectangles of different shades on the left side of the screen (deleting the sides to reduce clutter), then blending the middle object first to the dark, then to the light

Placing three rectangles of different shades on the right side of the screen (again, deleting the sides to reduce clutter), then blending the middle object first to the light, then to the dark

The final monitor screen in Preview

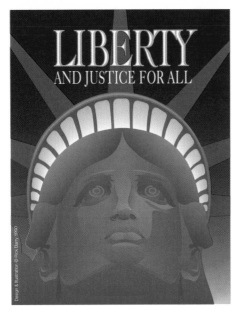
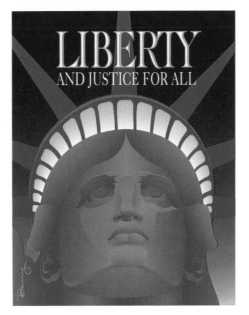

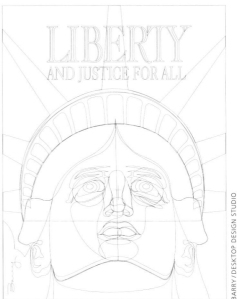

Gallery: Rick Barry / DeskTop Design Studio

To demonstrate the difference between blends and gradients, Rick Barry took an image he created with blends in Illustrator 3.2 (upper left Preview, lower left Artwork), selected the blends (by clicking twice with the Group-selection tool on one of the blend objects) and deleted them. The objects used to create the blends remained, and Barry filled these objects with custom gradients and then adjusted the rate and range of the gradients with the Gradient tool (upper right Preview, lower right Artwork).

Pathfinder & Other Filters

6

Pathfinder & Other Filters

Introduction...

Where did all the filters go?

Rather than always appearing in the Filter menu, plug-ins can now appear anywhere and look like just about anything:

- New **Plug-in tools** replace or supplement filters (also see ⑥): **Star**, **Polygon** and **Spiral** (see page 126); **Twirl** (page 124); and **Knife**, which performs Pathfinder-like Divide functions (see ⑥ for details on this quirky tool).
- **Text filters** are built into the Type menu (see page 136).
- The **Align** palette (Window menu) replaces Align and Distribute (see page 125).
- **Transform Each** (Arrange menu) replaces Move Each, Scale Each and Rotate Each (see page 125).
- **Document Info** is now logically placed in the File menu.

See the latest Illustrator and third-party manuals for new plug-ins!

Reopening the last filter

To reapply the last filter you used, select it from the top of the Filter menu (or ⌘-Shift-E). To reopen the last filter and change the settings, hold down the Option key and select it from the top of the menu (or Option-⌘-Shift-E).

You'll save a lot of time constructing images in Illustrator if you learn to use the Pathfinder and other plug-in filters, and this chapter should help you narrow down the guesswork. Because filters can irrevocably change your objects, limiting their editability, you should *always* work on *copies* of your objects in files that are backed up.

Instead of memorizing the filters, learn what effects and techniques are possible, then locate the filters most likely to result in the desired effect. If the filter doesn't work as expected, use Undo (⌘-Z) and try another. If you're pleased with the filter's effects, you'll want to choose Group (⌘-G) while the objects are still selected.

The exact plug-ins available to you will vary depending on your version of Illustrator, and which third-party plug-ins you use (see Tip at top left and the Plug-ins folder on the *Wow!* disk). The charts throughout this chapter demonstrate the results of Adobe and *Wow!* Illustrator filters as applied to simple geometric objects, and sometimes to *Wow!* artists' work as further explanation. Also, see the Plug-ins folder on the *Wow!* disk for printable charts detailing the settings for the more complex filters.

Use the versatile Select filters to automatically select similarly filled, stroked or styled objects. If you need to locate masks within an image (although this filter doesn't always find masks on separate layers), try Select: Select Masks to activate unlocked, visible masking objects (see *Chapter 4* for locking and layers, and *Chapter 8* for masks). Are you having trouble selecting all but a few objects? Select the few you don't want, then choose Select: Select Inverse. (If you need to invert a selection that includes *type*, hold down the Shift key and marquee the entire page to toggle your selection.) A wonderful filter is Select: Select Stray Points, which selects lone points so you can delete them before they cause big trouble (see Note below). Illustrator 6 filter Objects: Cleanup can also delete stray points, but beware—it could also delete

unstroked, unfilled objects that you may be using.
Note: *Selecting a lone point by accident can prevent you from Joining properly, or could even cause your objects to disappear if you choose to mask when a point is on top!*

PATHFINDER FILTERS

Outside of making sure you apply filters to copies and not originals, here are a few more tips for working with Pathfinder filters:

- **Reset Pathfinder Options**
  Illustrator 6 still requires you to reset Pathfinder Options each time you start your program. I reverse the settings from "Remove redundant points" to "Divide and Outline" in order to get colored, not unfilled, objects.

- **With most Pathfinder filters, the top color will be maintained.** With the notable exception of the Minus Front filter, which subtracts the front object from the back (keeping the back object's color), most Pathfinder filters that combine objects will result in an object the color of the topmost object. Be aware that some filters (such as Merge and Trim) delete the path strokes of your objects (another reason to keep originals). To maintain the color in objects for which you use Divide or Outline filters, reset Pathfinder Options (see paragraph above).

- **Make compound paths to run Pathfinder filters on multiple separate objects.** Some filters, such as Minus Front (or Minus Back), result in one single object, affected by all other objects. If, instead, you wish to maintain multiple separate objects that are affected by just one single object, copy the group of objects you want to have operate together and choose Object: Compound Paths: Make (⌘-8). All the objects will now be styled the same as the backmost object (if your objects overlap, see the tip at right) and will operate as a unit when you apply the filter. Then, use the Direct-selection tool and the Paint Style palette or Paint-bucket to fill individual objects.

Other people's plug-ins

Numerous third-party companies now provide a wide range of plug-in filters, tools and effects. See the Plug-ins folder on the *Wow!* disk for samples and demos!

What about the other filters?

See the following for more info:
- For Select filters, and Objects: Cleanup, see page 118.
- For a step-by-step lesson using Ink Pen and Path Pattern see ⑥ (a Gallery of this on page 129).
- For Text filters, see *Chapter 7*.
- For Filter: Other: Overprint Black, see Tip on page 55.
- For Pathfinder: Trap, see pages 21 and 64, *Chapters 1* and *3*.
- For Other: Make Riders/Delete Riders, see the *User Guide*.

Avoiding compound drop-out

When you create a compound path of multiple ob-jects (see "Make compound paths" at left), the back   object will "drop out" as white where it overlaps other objects. To avoid this, temporarily add another object and choose Arrange: Send To Back. Select the original objects along with the new backmost object and press ⌘-8. Then use the Direct-selection tool to select and delete this extra reversing object and proceed with your image.

Pathfinder Filters

The default settings for 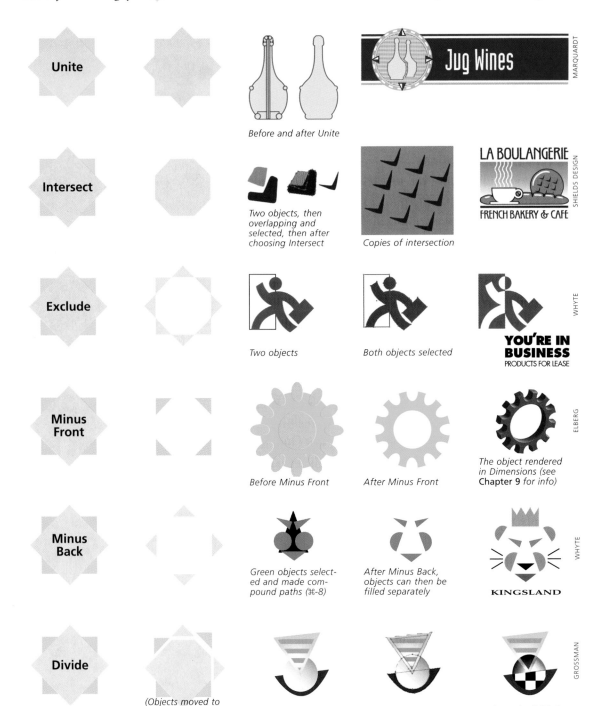 *were used unless otherwise noted. Artists' work may use custom settings.*

Unite

Before and after Unite

Intersect

Two objects, then overlapping and selected, then after choosing Intersect

Copies of intersection

Exclude

Two objects

Both objects selected

Minus Front

Before Minus Front

After Minus Front

The object rendered in Dimensions (see Chapter 9 for info)

Minus Back

Green objects selected and made compound paths (⌘-8)

After Minus Back, objects can then be filled separately

Divide

(Objects moved to show results)

Four objects

Objects divided

Each newly divided object filled

Pathfinder Filters (continued)

The default settings for *were used unless otherwise noted. Artists' work may use custom settings.*

Outline

*(Objects moved and line weights **increased** to .5-pt to show results)*

Before Outline

After Outline, and resetting line weight

Trim

(Objects moved to show results)

Before Trim; in Preview and Artwork

After Trim; overlaps are reduced, BUT strokes are lost

Merge

(Objects moved to show results)

Before Merge in Artwork

After Merge; like fills are united, BUT strokes are lost

Crop

A copy of the fish in front to use for Crop

After Crop; objects are now separated

Hard

Same color objects don't mix, so over-lapping objects were colored differently

After Hard filter; Each overlap is now a separate object

After using the Eyedropper to switch the colors in the front objects

Soft

Before Soft filter; the blue wave overlaps the detail along the bottom of the rocks

After Soft filter (see SandeeC's Mix soft Tip in the Illustrator 5 Goodies archive on the Wow! disk)

Practical Path-cuts

Preparing for Blends with Pathfinder Filters

Overview: *Use a bisecting path with Divide; combine drawn elements and copies using Unite; create see-through details using Exclude.*

Pathfinder filters can be astounding time-savers for creating realistic renderings. To form the basic shapes then used for photorealistic blends, Thomas Neal (of Thomas • Bradley Illustration & Design) used to painstakingly cut and join the paths using the Scissors tool with Average and Join (see page 10 for cutting and joining, and pages 112 and 162 to see the resulting blends). Pathfinder filters practically automate Neal's tasks for preparing basic objects to use for blending. (See *Chapter 4* for help with hiding, locking and reordering objects.)

1

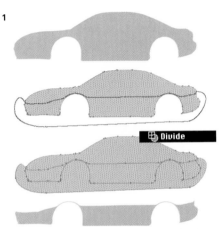

An object; drawing a bisecting path; selecting and dividing; extraneous objects deleted

2

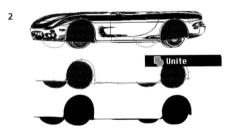

Drawing a fender-well; selecting it with copies of tires to unite; the final path united

3

The outer portion of the wiper and drawing the inner objects; selecting them both to exclude

1 Using Divide to create a subsection of your car. Copy the object that defines your car body, Lock it (⌘-1) and use Paste In Front to paste a copy exactly on top. Using the Pen tool, draw a path bisecting the car, then loop the path around to create a closed path surrounding the car so that the only place where the car can be divided is along your bisecting path. Select both objects and choose Filter: Pathfinder: Divide, then delete the extraneous objects.

2 Using Unite to create your undercarriage. Using the Pen tool, draw a path that defines the shadow in the fender-wells. Copy and Paste In Front the four wheels, and use ⌘-G to group them. With the Shift key, select the fender-wells with the grouped wheels and choose Filter: Pathfinder: Unite.

3 Creating see-through details. Create an object that forms the outline of your wiper. Using filled black objects, draw the areas you want to cut out of the outline. Select the outer and inner objects and choose Filter: Pathfinder: Exclude.

KLINE/ACME DESIGN

Gallery: Michael Kline / Acme Design

When Michael Kline uses Pathfinder filters, he always uses a copy of the object in case he needs that object again for something else. With this illustration for Kids Discover *magazine, Kline kept an earlier version of the house handy so that, if he needed to, he could quickly copy the original and use Paste In Front to place that into the working version.*

For the lines in the roof, Kline used the Brush tool, set at 2.5 points, 130° calligraphic angle, and 60% black. Once all the lines were drawn, he used Pathfinder: Crop to "cookie-cut" the basic shape of the roof. He used the same treatment for most of the siding. (The bushes were given a random look with the calligraphic Brush tool in varying shades of green, then "ruffled" using Distort: Roughen.) Kline also used Pathfinder filters in the "cookie-cutting" of objects into other objects. He did almost all the detail in the shadows using Pathfinder: Soft at varying percentages—again, using a copy of all his objects to retain the integrity of originals in case he needed to reuse them.

Distort Filters and Stylize Filters

Note: *See the Plug-ins folder and* ⑥ *on the* **Wow!** *disk for charts and lessons for some of these filters.*

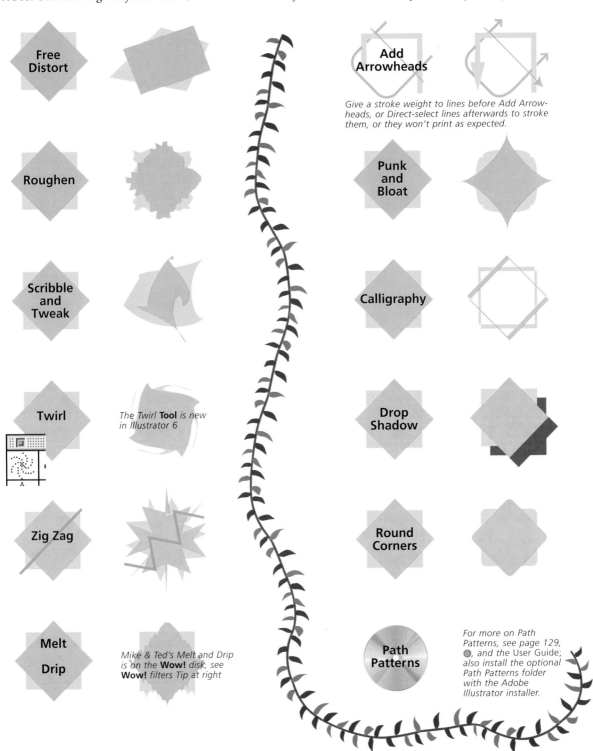

Free Distort

Roughen

Scribble and Tweak

Twirl

The Twirl **Tool** *is new in Illustrator 6*

Zig Zag

Melt Drip

Mike & Ted's Melt and Drip is on the **Wow!** *disk, see* **Wow!** *filters Tip at right*

Add Arrowheads

Give a stroke weight to lines before Add Arrowheads, or Direct-select lines afterwards to stroke them, or they won't print as expected.

Punk and Bloat

Calligraphy

Drop Shadow

Round Corners

Path Patterns

For more on Path Patterns, see page 129, ⑥, and the User Guide; also install the optional Path Patterns folder with the Adobe Illustrator installer.

Objects Filters, Ink Pen, Align, Transform Each

The Ink Pen filter

The Ink Pen is a wonderfully powerful filter that can generate random textured fills and cross-hatch pen-like shading techniques. There are numerous Ink Pen settings, so be prepared to experiment a bit in order to achieve the desired results. See ⑥ for a step-by-step technique using Ink Pen (a Gallery of that image is on page 129—detail at right); also see the Plug-ins folder on the *Wow!* disk for art samples using the Ink Pen (such as Sandee Cohen's "Veggie Burger" at top right), and Victor von Salza's Ink Pen Goodie.

COHEN (on the *Wow!* disk)

detail from page 129

Add Anchor Points

This filter adds one Anchor Point between every 2 existing anchor points (to repeat ⌘-Option-E).

Offset Path

Don't use this filter! It creates excess points and can create excess objects! Instead, use **SCT Inset Path***, see below*

Outline Path

Original line in Artwork, then after Outline Path

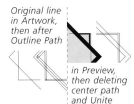

in Preview, then deleting center path and Unite

Scale To Dimension Wow!

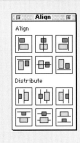

On the **Wow!** *disk, see* **Wow!** *Tip at right*

SCT Inset Path

2-pt Inset

On the **Wow!** *disk, see* **Wow!** *Tip at right*

Smart Remove Points

before   after

On the **Wow!** *disk, see* **Wow!** *Tip at right*

Align palette (Window menu)

Use the Align palette to perform these former Objects filter functions: Align Objects, Distribute Horizontally, and Distribute Vertically. Because this is a palette, if you don't like the result, just Undo and try again.

Be careful with Transform Each (Arrange menu)

This dialog box combines the former Objects filters: Move Each, Rotate Each and Scale Each. Be careful, however, because *each* object transforms about its own center—even if it's grouped with other objects. Enable the Preview, and try Random for some fun!

Installing the *Wow!* filters

Melt and Drip, Scale To Dimension, SCT Inset Path, and Smart Remove Points filters are in the Plug-ins folder on the *Wow!* disk; place them in the Plug-ins folder in *your* Illustrator folder and relaunch Illustrator.

Create Filters, Plug-in tools: Polygon, Spiral, Star

See page 124 (Distort filters) for the Twirl tool, and see ⑥ for details on the Knife tool.

FIll & Stroke for Mask

Stroke for Mask

Fill for Mask

WANG, SZUJEWSKA / ADOBE

Mosaic

Select an embedded image object, and choose Filter: Create: Mosaic
(To use Mosaic in Illustrator 5, see **Chapter 9**, *page 185)*

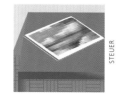

STEUER

You should group a mosaic immediately

Trim Marks

Trim marks at left have been greatly reduced in size (for more info on trim marks and crop-marks, see Tip on page 147)

Polygon

GROSSMAN

Spiral

GROSSMAN

Star

TINKEL

Applying stubborn filters

If you get a low-memory message, or if a filter just doesn't work, try these options, in order: 1) saving, 2) closing extra files, 3) quitting other open applications, 4) running the filter in a new file (using Copy and Paste In Front to maintain registration), 5) relaunching Illustrator, 6) allocating more RAM to Illustrator (see pages 2–3).

Serious fun with the Polygon, Spiral and Star

The Polygon, Spiral and Star are deceptively powerful tools in disguise. Used in conjunction with the following key combinations, these timesaving tools are likely to become indispensable:

- **Spacebar-drag** allows you to reposition your object.
- **Shift** constrains the object's proportions.
- **Up-arrow** (↑) increases points on a star, sides on a polygon, and winds on a spiral.
- **Down-arrow** (↓) removes points from a star, sides from a polygon, and winds from a spiral.
- **Option** aligns shoulders (arms) on a star.
- **Control-drag** changes the inside/outside radius of a star, or increases or decreases the "decay" in a spiral.
- **W** (the "W" key) will produce offsets of your object. Try combining the W key with the Spacebar for a cool trailing objects effect!
- **Option-click** to create the object numerically.
- **Various combinations of the above:** Try experimenting with all the keys separately, and also in combination with the other keys. Actually, playing with the modifier keys as you draw is the only way to really understand these fun and powerful tools.

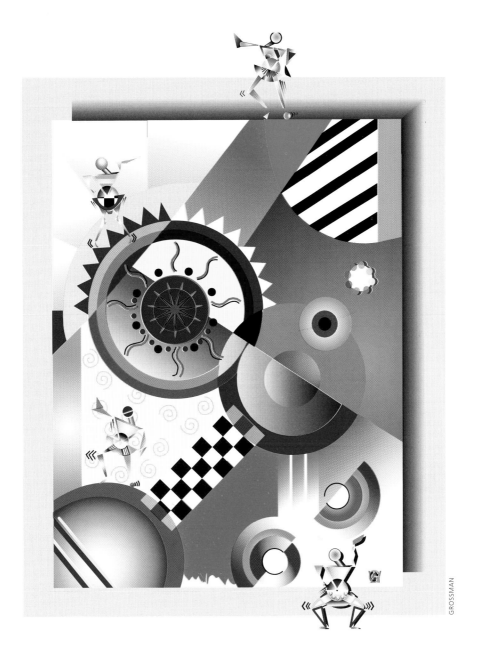

Gallery: Wendy Grossman

Wendy Grossman was inspired by the prospect of a Wow! filters chapter and spent a weekend playing with the filters to create this cubist image. She used the Pathfinder: Unite filter to frequently combine multiple objects. She used the Pathfinder: Divide filter to segment objects into smaller, discrete objects, and the Pathfinder: Soft filter for blending colors between objects (such as the 70% Soft filter used in the "color wheel"). The Create filters which are easy to see are the Star and Spiral filters.

Colors Filters

Important: *Before using Colors filters, see Tip directly below; and for lines, use Object: Outline Path.*

Adjust Colors

Start with Adjust Colors to convert Custom colors to Process colors

Since many filters and gradients don't work on Custom colors, use Adjust Colors with the Convert: Custom to Process option before applying other filters. (In Illustrator 5, use the "Optional" Convert Custom to Process filter.)

Saturate

Artistically adjusting colors with Adjust Colors and Saturate

Use Adjust Colors and Saturate to change colors in complex object groups such as path pattern, ink pen, and even image objects (see Gallery opposite, and ⑥). In Illustrator 6, simply move sliders, checking the Preview box to see possible results. (Illustrator 5's Adjust Colors requires you to click Apply after each increase/decrease, typing a zero into fields you no longer want to change; Saturate is separated into four separate filters.)

Invert Colors

Note: Blacks and blends don't invert

Recoloring blends with the Colors: Blend filters

Use Blend filters to make color changes to multiple objects; this technique is especially useful for recalculating colors within a blend after changing end colors!

Blend Front to Back

Blended objects (process colors only!)

First and last blend objects recolored

After Blend Front to Back

Blend Horizontally

A blend with new colors on each end, then all selected

After Blend Horizontally with the new end colors

Blend Vertically

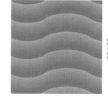

A blend, then with new colors on top and bottom

After Blend Vertically with the new top and bottom colors

Gallery: Sharon Steuer *(see ⑥ for the full step-by-step technique using this image)*
All of the foliage in this illustration was created by applying one of five Path Pattern tiles
to freeform paths drawn with the Pen tool. For objects that would "grow" on either side of
a path (such as vines and clusters of leaves), I designed horizontal pattern tiles; for asym-
metrical patterns running along only one side of the path (like ferns and grass), the tiles
were designed vertically. I defined the boundary of each pattern tile with an unstroked,
unfilled rectangle below, then selected the tile (and bounding rectangle) and chose Object:
Pattern and New to name the selected pattern. To create the path patterns, I drew a path
(or a group of paths) and chose Filter: Stylize: Path Pattern, loaded the desired pattern
under "Sides" and clicked OK. Color variations were achieved by selecting a group of path pattern
objects (with the Selection tool) and applying Filter: Colors: Adjust Colors, or Filter: Colors: Saturate.

Fanciful Filtering
Creative Experimentation With Filters

Advanced Technique

Overview: *Create objects as the basis for filtering; use various filters on different groups of objects; make color and object adjustments as necessary.*

The template with grid before and after the first ovals and lines are drawn and text is placed

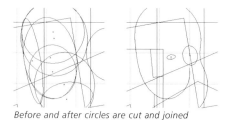

Before and after circles are cut and joined

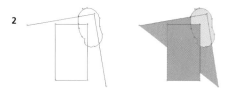

Three objects selected in Artwork and Preview

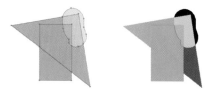

The Soft filter applied, then objects recolored

A wonderful way to learn new techniques is through creative experimentation. When Ron Chan was commissioned to create artwork for the University of Minnesota, he used the opportunity to experiment with filters. Don't forget that many different ways exist to achieve the same effect, and you might gravitate towards an entirely different set of filters.

1 Preparing your basic objects from which to work.
Create the objects that will form the basis for your filtering. Chan used methods discussed elsewhere in the book to prepare the initial objects, including scanning a sketch to use as a template (page 80), creating a custom drawing grid (see Tip on page 137) in its own layer (page 96) and making a masking layer (page 152). He also cut and joined circles to form the head (page 52). In final preparation for filtering, Chan drew bisecting lines with the Pen tool, which he later used as guides in applying filters.

2 Selecting overlapping objects and applying the Pathfinder: Soft filter. After creating a few overlapping objects, you might choose to see how those objects "cut into" each other. First, select the objects with any selection tool (you can even select part of an object using the Direct-selection tool). Although you can use Pathfinder: Divide to create separate objects for each point where the objects intersect, Chan prefers to use the Pathfinder: Soft filter, because the Soft filter creates new colors where objects overlap, making the intersections easy to see. He can then recolor like-colored objects as a unit by Direct-selecting one color and using the Select: Select Same Fill Color filter, which selects all objects of that color. Chan also uses Direct-select on particular divided objects for recoloring individually.

3 Offsetting and outlining paths. To create an offset of a path, choose Filter: Objects: Offset Path and specify how much larger or smaller the offset path should be. Chan offset the jaw path smaller at −6 points, used Direct-select on the original and offset paths' endpoints to join (⌘-J) them and then filled the new joined object. Since strokes can't contain gradients or patterns (see *Chapter 5* for gradients; *Chapter 3* for patterns), use Filter: Objects: Outline Path to convert stroked paths into filled objects that can be styled with more flexibility.

4 Cropping copies for an overlay look. To create a transparent overlay look in a section of your image, first select and copy all the objects that will be affected. Then deselect everything (Shift-⌘-A), and use Paste In Front (⌘-F) and Group (⌘-G) on the copy. Using any tools you wish, create a closed object to define your cropping area and, with your Shift key down, use the Selection tool to select the grouped copy and its cropping object; then choose Filter: Pathfinder: Crop and group the cropped objects. Try experimenting with the Colors: Adjust Colors filter to see if you can achieve a color cast you like (see page 188). Or, just Direct-select objects to customize their styling. ⟳

Filter: Pathfinder: Soft options

In addition to letting you choose the color mixing percentage, the

Soft filter also lets you convert custom colors to process. If you disable this option, then overlapping custom colors won't mix at all; they'll merely divide.

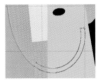

Before and after offsetting the path −6 points

Joining the two paths and then changing style

Lines selected, then outlined, then customized

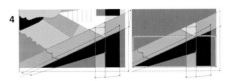

Objects copied, then after Paste In Front and being selected with a defining rectangle

After Pathfinder: Crop, then recolored

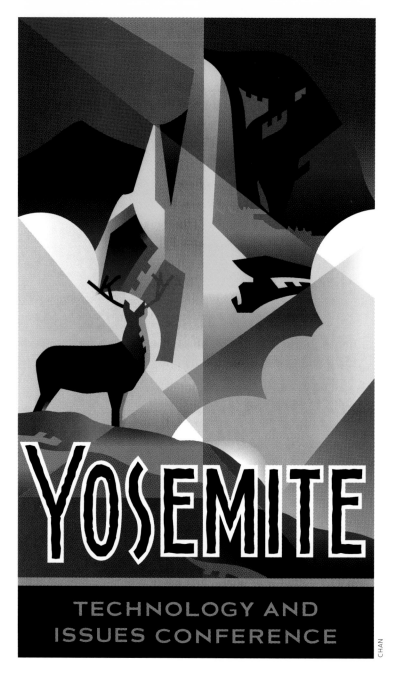

Gallery: Ron Chan

In very much the same way he made the image for the University of Minnesota discussed on the previous two pages, Ron Chan created this poster for a Yosemite conference. For the general composition, Chan used Soft, Outline Path, Offset Path and Crop filters. He used Type: Create Outlines to convert the "Yosemite" title to Bézier objects filled white, then used Offset Path, filled the inner offset objects with black and applied the Roughen filter.

Type & Layout

7

Type & Layout

Introduction...

The Type tool, Area-Type tool, Path-Type tool

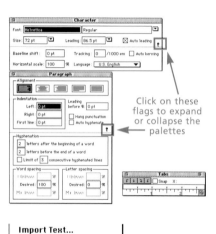

Click on these flags to expand or collapse the palettes

Import Text...

Selecting text or objects?

Once you've entered your text, you can use the Type tool to select any type element by clicking and dragging across letters, words or lines, double-clicking to select a word or Shift-clicking to extend a selection. If the text-insertion I-beam is activated, then Edit: Select All (⌘-A) selects all type within that text object. If your text I-beam is not activated, then Select All selects *all unlocked objects* in your image.

Illustrator is a powerful tool for controlling type graphically. Although you're likely to prefer a page-layout program (such as QuarkXPress or PageMaker) for multipage documents, this chapter will show you many reasons to stay within Illustrator for single-page documents, especially those pages that incorporate graphic elements. The Type chapter of Adobe's *User Guide* covers the creation and manipulation of type in great detail, so this introduction will focus on essentials and production tips.

For creating and manipulating type, there are two palettes you can open from the Window menu: Show Character (⌘-T; think "T for Type") and Show Paragraph (Shift-⌘-P). When you first select these palettes, they appear in a collapsed view. To see all options, expand the palette by clicking on the "flag" in the lower right.

There are a number of different type options in Illustrator: *Point Type, Area Type* and *Path Type*. The flexible Type tool lets you click to create a Point-Type object, click-drag to create an Area-Type object, or click within any existing type object to enter or edit text, or gain access to File: Import Text.

Select letters, words or an entire block of text by dragging across the letters with the Type tool, or use a selection tool to select text as an *object* by clicking on or marqueeing the type's baseline (the baseline is the line that type sits upon, and is visible in Artwork mode).

- **Point Type.** Click with the Type tool anywhere on the page to create Point Type. Once you click, a blinking text-insertion cursor called an "I-beam" indicates you can now type text using the keyboard. To add another line, press the Return key. When you're finished typing into one text object, click on the Type tool in the toolbox to simultaneously select the current text as an object (the I-beam will disappear) and be poised to begin another text object. To just select the text as an object, click on a selection tool.

- **Area Type.** If, instead of clicking, you click-drag with the Type tool, you'll create an Area-Type rectangle, into which you can type. Once your rectangle has been defined by the Type tool, the I-beam will await your typing, and the text will automatically wrap to the next line when you type to the confines of the rectangle. If you've typed more text than can fit in your text rectangle, then, in Artwork mode, you'll notice a plus sign along the right side of the rectangle. To enlarge the rectangle to allow for more text, use the Direct-select tool to deselect the text block, then grab one side of the rectangle and drag it out, holding down the Shift key to constrain the direction of the drag. To add a new text object that will be linked to an existing text object in Artwork mode, use the Group-select tool to grab the rectangle only (not the text), hold down the Option key and drag a copy of the rectangle. Text will automatically flow to the new rectangle.

The other way to create Area Type is to construct a path (with any tools you wish) forming a shape within which to place type. Then choose the Area-Type tool (click and hold down on the Type tool to access it) and click on the path itself to place text within the path. Distort the confining shape by grabbing an anchor point with the Direct-selection tool and dragging it to a new location, or reshape the path by adjusting direction lines. The text within will reflow.

To set up tabs for Area Type, choose Window: Show Tab Ruler. To create paths for custom tab alignment, first create paths that align with the tab markers, then Direct-select your text object with your paths and choose Type: Make Wrap. You can also use text-wrapping to flow text around objects (see the *User Guide*). After paths are wrapped to text objects, reshaping the paths causes text to reflow. To add a new path, ungroup (⌘-U) the current text and path objects, then reselect the text with the old and new paths and choose Make Wrap. (For more information about working with tabs, see the *User Guide*.)

Note: *You'll have to use Type: Release Wrap or Ungroup before you can apply some filters to wrapped text.*

Linking multiple text blocks

To link multiple text objects so that text flows from one to the next, select the desired text blocks with the Selection tool and choose Type: Link Blocks (⌘-Shift-G).

The quick-changing Type tool

When using the regular Type tool, look at your cursor very carefully in these situations:

- If you move the regular Type tool over a closed path, the cursor should change to the Area-Type icon.

- If you move the Type tool over an open path, it will probably change to the Path-Type icon.

- But, if the path is almost closed, you might get either the Area-Type or the Path-Type icon.

Typographic controls

Open General Preferences to set the default typographic controls accessible from your keyboard. Look under "Type" in the 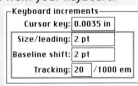 Adobe *Quick Reference Card* to learn the keyboard shortcuts for adjusting your kerning / tracking, leading, point sizes, baseline shifts and justification.

To create the illusion that type is falling along both the top and bottom of a path, hold down the Option key as you flip the I-beam: this action flips a *copy* of the type.

Reselect the Type tool to end one text object; the next click will start a new text object. Or, deselect the current text by holding down the ⌘ key (temporarily turning your cursor into a selection tool) and clicking outside the text block.

If you're missing fonts, don't be afraid to open the file, make changes, save, copy, paste the missing type or resave the file, because Illustrator remembers which fonts you're *supposed* to be using. However, the file won't print correctly until you load or replace the missing fonts (see "More about Find Font" at right).

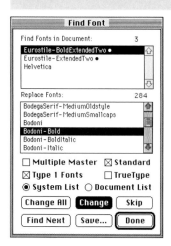

- **Path Type.** The Path-Type tool allows you to click on a path to flow text along the perimeter of the path (the path will then become unstroked/unfilled; also, see "Revert Text Path" below). To reposition the beginning of the text, use a Selection tool to grab the special Path-Type I-beam *itself* and drag left or right. Drag the I-beam up or down (or double-click it) to *flip* the text so it wraps along the inside or outside of the path (also see the top Tip at left).

  As with Area Type, use the Direct-selection tool to re-shape the confining path itself; the Path Type path will automatically readjust to the new path shape. 🔘

FILTERS FOR TEXT (Additional Type Functions)

Although in 5.5 the functions listed in this section were found under Filter: Text, in Illustrator 6 most of them are now incorporated into the Type menu.

- **Change Case** and **Export** filters require you to select with the Type tool before you use the filter.

- **Revert Text Path** transforms a text path into a regular Illustrator object path. Use of this filter requires you to have a text path selected with a Selection tool and no text associated with the path. (Illustrator 6.0 didn't ship with this filter, but it should be available from Adobe.)

- **Check Spelling**, **Find Font**, **Find** and **Smart Punctuation** all work whether or not anything is selected, although some of these filters give you the option to work within a selected text block if you have one selected.

More about Find Font: If you try to open a file and don't have the correct fonts loaded, Illustrator warns you, lists the missing fonts and asks if you still want to open the file. You need the correct fonts to print properly, so if you *can't* load the missing fonts, choose Find Font to find and replace the missing fonts with fonts you do have.

  When you open the filter, the top list displays the fonts used in the file; the missing fonts will be indicated by a "bullet" (•). In order to access all fonts that can be used as replacements, deselect the options you *don't* want to use (e.g., TrueType), then click System List and wait. If you click as the list is building, you'll interrupt the search and only have access to those fonts already found (you'll then have to click on the System button *again* to rebuild the list). When you're ready to select font replacements, click on the fonts you'd like to replace from the top list; note that Illustrator shows where the font occurs. After you choose a replacement font from the bottom list, you can individually replace each occurrence of the font by clicking Change and then clicking Find Next, or else simply click Change All to change all occurrences of the top fonts with the font selected from the bottom list. Holding down the Shift key allows you to select multiple fonts to replace, although you can select only one font at a time from the bottom list as a replacement.

About Rows & Columns: You can use Rows & Columns on any selected rectangle or Area Type. (Use a Selection tool, not the Type tool, to select the entire text object.) You can enter text first, or simply begin setting up your columns by choosing Rows & Columns. In this filter, specify the number and sizes of the rows and columns and whether you wish to use Add Guides. (This creates grouped lines that you can make into Illustrator guides with Object: Make Guides; see also page 96 for more on guides.) Keep Preview checked to see the results of your specifications while you work, and click Text Flow to choose whether text will flow horizontally or vertically from one block to another. ◔

Making object-drawing grids

Use Illustrator's type controls to make a custom drawing grid:

- In a new document, set the ruler units for your grid (in General Preferences).
- From the upper left corner of where you want your grid to begin, use your Type tool to drag out a small rectangle.
- Click on the Selection tool to activate the rectangle (instead of the text elements) and choose Rows & Columns. Set your total width and height to whole numbers that fit within your page. Type "0" for both gutters and set the number of rows and columns based on your total box height and width. (E.g., if your box is 8" by 10", specify 8 columns by 10 rows for a 1" grid, or 16 by 20 for a .5" grid.)
- Enable the Add Guides check box and click OK.
- Use the Selection tool to click on one guide (which selects them all) and choose Object: Guides: Make. Then choose Edit: Select All and delete the text objects.

—*Tip inspired by Sean McKenna.*

Choose your words, and letters, carefully!

Just having access to dozens of fonts doesn't make you a type expert, any more than having a handful of pens makes you an artist. Play all you want, but if you need professional typographic results, consult a professional. I did. Barbara Sudick designed this book.

Graphically transforming Bézier curves (artwork by Javier Romero Design Group)

Filling with patterns or gradients

Masking with the type (artwork by Min Wang / Adobe Systems)

Transporting foreign or unusual fonts (artwork by Kathleen Tinkel)

Using pre-Illustrator 5.5 vertically scaled type (artwork by Pamela Drury Wattenmaker)

CONVERTING TYPE TO OUTLINES

As long as you've created your type with fonts you have and can print, and provided you've finished experimenting with text as type elements (e.g., adjusting your line spacing or kerning/tracking, or wrapping text around a path), you have the option to convert your text objects to Illustrator Bézier curves with compound paths. Compound paths form the "holes" in objects, such as the transparent center of an "O" or "P." You can use the Direct-selection tool to select and manipulate parts of the compound paths separately. To convert a font to outlines, select the type with a Selection tool and choose Type: Create Outlines, and, while the type is still selected, choose Object: Group (⌘-G) to group the individual elements for easy reselection.

Why convert type to outlines?

• **So you can graphically transform or distort the individual curves and anchor points of letters or words.** Everything from the minor stretching of a word to extreme distortion is possible.

• **So you can fill type with patterns or gradients.**

• **So you can make type into a masking object.** See page 140 for an example of this technique.

• **So you don't have to supply the font to your client or service bureau.** Converting type can be especially useful when you're using foreign language fonts, or when your image will be printed when you're not around.

• **So you can work with vertically scaled type created before Illustrator 5.5.** Illustrator 5.5 computes vertical scaling of type differently from that of earlier versions, so if you want to work with type that was vertically scaled in an earlier version of Illustrator, select the type immediately after opening the file, and convert it to outlines; otherwise, you'll have to re-transform the type.

Gallery: James Young / Adobe Systems, Inc.

This alphabet (which would have been a nightmare to create in QuarkXPress or PageMaker) was simple to construct in Illustrator. James Young arranged individual Point-Type letters using the Selection tool and resized each visually using the Scale tool with the Shift-key down (to constrain scaling to proportionate only; see page 38 for scaling help). Because Young created this graphic using the Nueva Multiple Master (MM) font, he was able to select letters to change their width and weight (see page 142 for more on MM fonts).

YOUNG/ADOBE SYSTEMS, INC.

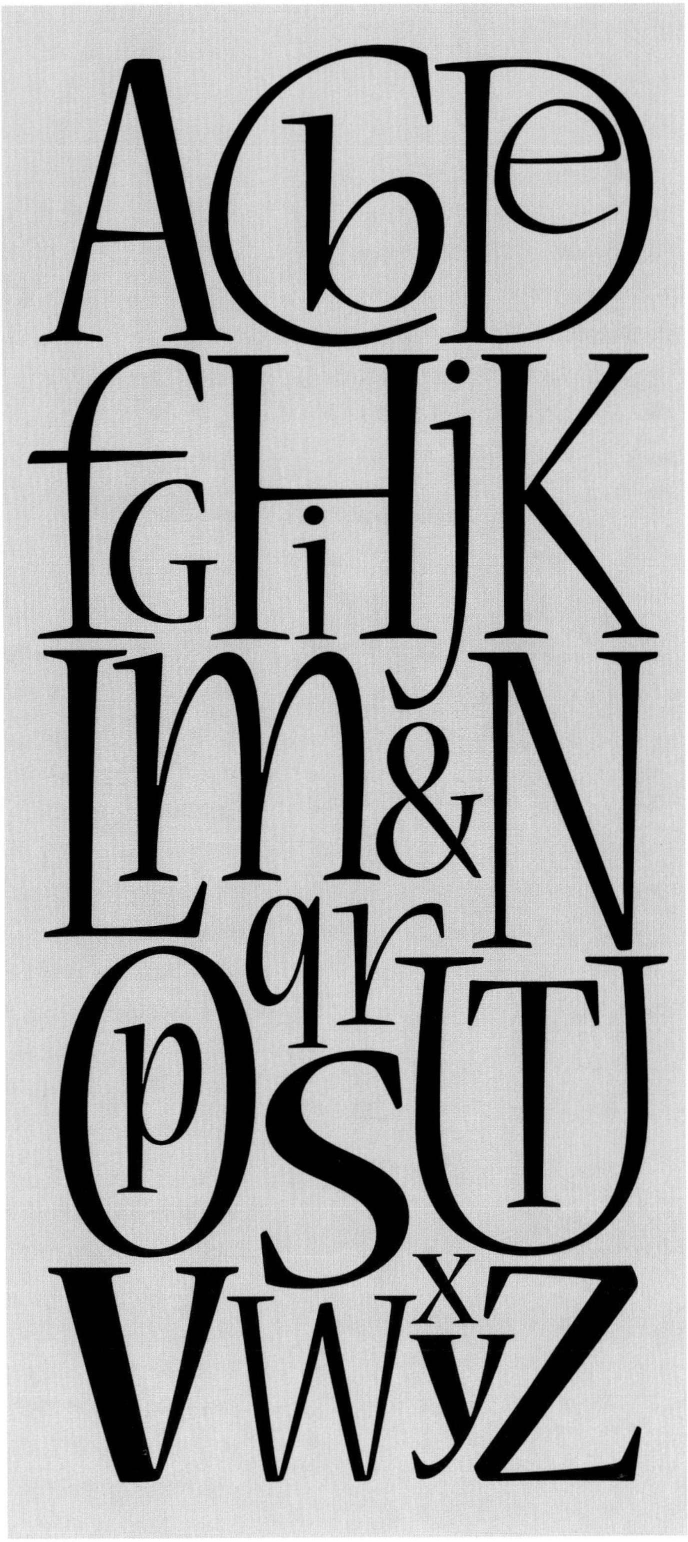

Masking Type

Placing Type Within Type Using Masks

Overview: *Create a large letter and arrange other objects in relation to the letter; convert the large letter to outlines; bring the outlined letter to the front and make it into a mask for the other objects; use the Create: Fill & Stroke for Mask filter.*

1

Arranged type objects and the "M" outlined

2

"M" brought to front and all objects selected

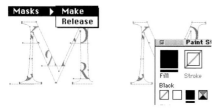

"M" masked, then only the mask selected with a paint style chosen

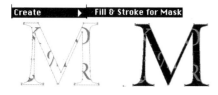

Before and after Filter: Create: Fill & Stroke for Mask is applied

This "M" was created by Min Wang (Laurie Szujewska, art director) for the Minion type specimen book. Illustrator 5.5's new masking technique and a special mask filter simplified what would have been a longer process.

1 Positioning type elements and converting the large letter to outlines. Using the Type tool, click to create a Point-Type object and type one letter. Choose a typeface of a heavy enough weight and in a large enough size for other elements to show through the letter form itself. Then arrange other type elements (or other objects) in relation to the large letter (you'll be able to move them later). Wang arranged separate Minion type characters in relation to a 297-pt "M." Select the large letter with a Selection tool and choose Type: Create Outlines.

2 Creating the mask and "filling" it. Select the outline "M" and bring it to the front (⌘-=), then select all objects and apply Object: Mask: Make. Direct-select individual objects to adjust their placement. To create the illusion that the mask is filled or stroked (masks never actually receive fill or stroke), select the mask only, choose the desired paint style (you'll get a warning if you forget) and use Filter: Create: Fill & Stroke for Mask to create new filled or stroked objects within the mask. ✐

Gallery: Laurie Szujewska / Adobe Systems, Inc.

For Adobe's Poetica type specimen book, Laurie Szujewska was inspired by a "love knot" poem from the book Pattern Poetry *by Dick Higgins, and created a similar spiral path with the Pen tool. She used the Path-Type tool to place the text on the path. She then meticulously kerned and placed spaces along the type path to prevent text overlaps, and to get things just right.*

Gallery: Laurie Szujewska / Adobe Systems, Inc.

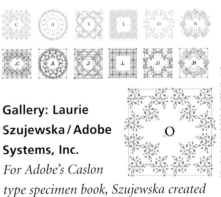

For Adobe's Caslon type specimen book, Szujewska created these decorative ornaments by placing, rotating and reflecting groups of separate Point-Type objects filled with a gray color.

The Shape of Time

Trickling Type with Variations of Type Style

Overview: *Create the outside border and path baselines for your type; import text into the first line; cut and paste text into appropriate path lines, changing the typestyle each time; use Point Type for "trickling type" and baseline shifts for lines at the bottom.*

To illustrate the effects of varying the weight and width of a Multiple Master (MM) typeface, James Young (with Laurie Szujewska) created this interpretation of George Kubler's *The Shape of Time*. If you don't have a MM font, modify this technique to vary type *sizes* using any typeface—or buy Minion MM from Adobe at a *Wow!* price of $39 (call 1-800-521-1976 and give ID# P-58-17-6).

1

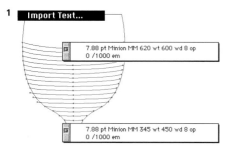

1 Creating your baselines. Draw an hourglass-shaped path with the Pen tool (see page 4 for help), and decide on a starting type size and style. Set your leading between lines one point larger than your type. Just move copies of your path *up* a distance equal to your leading; select the path, Option-click the Selection tool, specify a Move equal to the desired leading, and click Copy. Then ⌘-D to make copies for each line of type. Young started with Minion MM Bold Extended at 7.88 points , with 8.88-pt leading, and 18 lines of type. To cut the paths to fit the hourglass, copy the hourglass, select the paths and Paste In Front (⌘-F) a copy. Shift-select the paths with this hourglass copy and choose Filter: Pathfinder: Outline, then select and delete the paths outside the hourglass.

2

Weight

(Bold - Light)	÷ (# of steps -1)	▼
(620 - 345)	÷ (17) =	16
Line 1		620
Line 2	620 - 16 =	604
Line 3	604 - 16 =	588
...		

Width

(Extended - Condensed)	÷ (# of steps -1)	▼
(600 - 450)	÷ (17) =	8.8
Line 1		600
Line 2	600 - 8.8 =	591.2
Line 3	591.2 - 8.8 =	582.4
...		

Size

(12-point - 6-point)	÷	▼
	÷ (17) =	.35
Line 1		12
Line 2	12 - .35 =	11.65
Line 3	11.65 - .35 =	11.30
...		

2 Preparing your type. In a word processor, thoroughly proofread and spell-check your text, as making changes later will be difficult. Next, calculate and write down the variations in style to be placed on each path line, using the chart at left for help. Each of the MM typestyles has a numeric value that you'll be using for calculations (for size changes, use point sizes instead of the weight and width values). For the top line of type, Young used Bold Extended with a weight value of 620 and a width value of 600, and for the bottom, a Light Condensed with a weight of 345 and a width of 450. To calculate the weight and width

The number of ways for things to occupy time is probably no more unlimited than the large number of ways in which matter occupies space. The difficulty with delimiting the categories of time has always been to find a suitable description of duration, which would vary according to events while measuring them against a fixed scale. History has no periodic table of elements, and no classification of types or species; it has only solar time and a few old ways of grouping events, but no theory of temporal structure. If any principle of classing events be preferred to the impossible conception that every event will cluster during a given portion of time in an order varying between dense and sparse array. The classes we are considering contain events related as progressive solutions to problems of which the requirements are modified by each successive solution. A rapid succession of events is a dense array; a slow succession with many interruptions is sparse. In the history of art it occasionally happens that one generation, and even one individual achieves many new positions not only in one sequence but in a whole set of sequences. At the other extreme a given need will subsist for generations or even centuries without fresh solutions. We have already examined these occurrences under the heading of fast and slow happening. They have been explained as contingent upon position in the series and upon the varying pace of invention in different centers of population. Let us now look at further varieties in the array of

YOUNG / SZUJEWSKA / ADOBE SYSTEMS, INC. with text from George Kubler's *The Shape of Time*

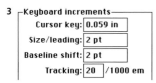

Changing the Cursor-key increments for typographic controls in General Preferences

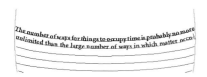

Cutting and pasting type into paths with the Path-Type tool

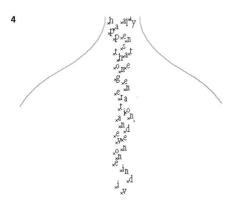

Trickling type using separate Point-Type objects

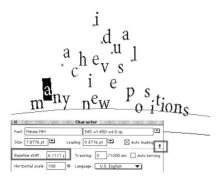

Graphically adjusting baseline shifts and viewing the shifts in the Character palette, which is hidden until you click the palette flag

values for each of the in-between steps, he subtracted the lowest value from the highest and divided it by the number of steps (18) minus 1. The resulting value (16 for weight and 8.8 for width) represented the size of the steps from one line of text to the next. Starting with Bold Extended at 620/600, Young subtracted 16 from 620 to get the weight of the second step (604), and 8.8 from 600 to get the width of the second step (591.2). He subtracted the same values from the second step to calculate the third, and so on.

3 Placing type into baselines. With your Path-Type tool, click on the top path and choose File: Import Text to place your text onto the path. Direct-select the text-insertion I-beam and drag it until the text begins just inside the hourglass. Then click with your Type cursor at the end of the word closest to the right side of the hourglass (add a hyphen if you must), press ⌘-Shift-Option-↓ to select all text beyond the line and cut the selected text. If necessary, place the Text cursor between words and kern slightly using Option-←/→ (set the Cursor-key distance in General Preferences). After adjusting the first line, click with the Path-Type tool on the second line and paste the cut text. Set the typestyle based on your "line 2" calculation, and repeat the above procedure until text is placed on all existing lines. Then click-drag to create an Area-Type object in which to paste the remaining text temporarily.

4 Creating the trickling type. Select and cut one letter at a time, then click within the hourglass to paste each letter as Point Type. Create the paths for the bottom of the hourglass, and calculate the values for increasing the weight/width (or size) of the styles. Click inside the temporary Area-Type object, press ⌘-A (Select All) and cut the text. With the Path-Type tool, place the text into the remaining paths at the bottom, placing fewer words just before the type hits the bottom. On these shorter lines, drag across individual letters with the Type tool and use Option-Shift-↑/↓ to create a baseline shift graphically. ◖

Gallery: Laurie Szujewska / Adobe Systems, Inc.

For the Adobe Caslon type specimen book, Laurie Szujewska created this reinterpretation of Lewis Carroll's handwritten, shaped poem from Alice's Adventures Underground. *Szujewska created the curved Bézier paths as described in "The Shape of Time" (page 142), but this time with a 14-pt distance for the leading and 28 duplications (⌘-D). After placing the appropriate text individually onto each line in 12-pt Adobe Caslon Italic (by clicking with the Path-Type cursor), Szujewska used the Direct-selection tool to adjust the angles of the curves. She then adjusted the starting point of each line of text by grabbing the I-beam and dragging it along the path. Finally, she individually selected each of the words in the last phrase (from "as he sat…") and progressively reduced them in size from "as he" at 11-pt to "Think of that!" at 6-pt.*

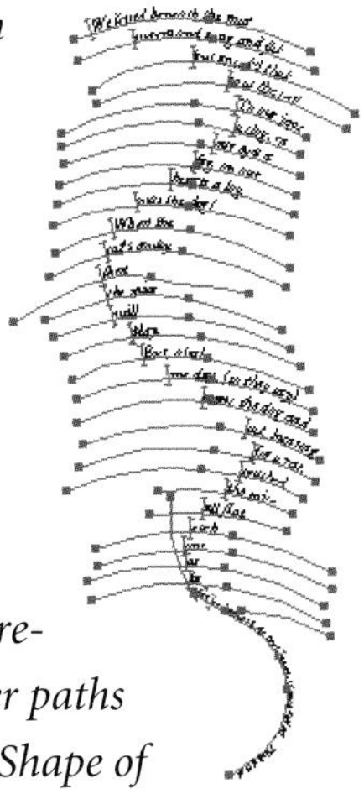

We lived beneath the mat
warm and snug and fat
but one, & that
was the cat!
To our joys
a clog, in
our eyes a
fog, on our
hearts a log,
was the dog!
When the
cat's away,
then
the mice
will
play.
But, alas!
one day, (so they say)
came the dog and
cat, hunting
for a rat,
crushed
the mice
all flat,
each
one
as
he
sat underneath the mat, warm, & snug and fat… Think of that!

Bookcover Design

Illustrator as a Stand-alone Layout Tool

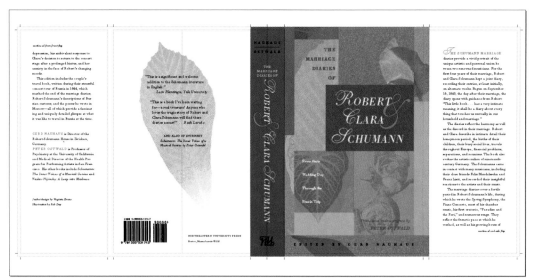

Overview: *Set your document size; place guides and cropmarks; place EPS files and make Area Type for columns and Point Type for graphic type; visually track type to fit.*

Page layout programs such as QuarkXPress and Page-Maker are essential for producing multipage, complex documents. However, Rob Day and Virginia Evans use Illustrator exclusively for their single-page design projects; for example, their book jacket designs.

1 Setting up your page. Choose File: Document Setup (⌘-Shift-D) to set up the Artboard for your design. Click on landscape or portrait page orientation and enter your Artboard size, making sure it's large enough for crop and/or registration marks (the "Size" parameter will automatically switch to "Custom"). Disable "Show placed images" to keep your Artwork view uncluttered (placed images will always show in Preview). Choose Show Rulers and "re-zero" your ruler origin to the upper left corner of where your page will begin (see page 20). Although you can generate uniform grids with the Rows & Columns filter (see page 137), for columns of varying sizes, Day and Evans numerically created two sets of rectangles, one for bleeds, and one for the trims. With the Rectangle tool (see page 8), click

Setting up the Artboard and layout specs

to make boxes sized for each trim area; Day and Evans made boxes for the front, side, flaps and spine. For bleeds, Option-click on the center of each trim area to numerically specify a box .125" larger in each dimension. To place an overall trim mark, select the boxes representing the entire trim area and choose Filter: Create: Trim Marks. If desired, make additional trim marks.

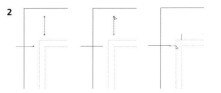

2 Customizing your guides. Select your trim and bleed boxes or columns (not the trim marks) and make them into guides (⌘-5), or Object: Guides: Make. (See page 96 for more on guides.) To shorten the trim marks, move the outside points inward until they touch the bleed guides (Direct-select an anchor point or Direct-select marquee multiple points and drag inward holding the Shift key).

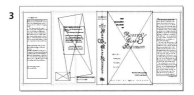

Shortening the trim marks; for folds, style with a dashed line (see page 54)

3 Placing the elements. Choose File: Place Art to select EPS images to import into your layout. Use Area Type to place columns of text into your layout grid; use Point Type to place lines of type and individual type elements. To track type visually to fit a space, select a text object and use Option-←/→. (See the intro to this chapter for tips on how to change text and typestyles using filters.) ◉

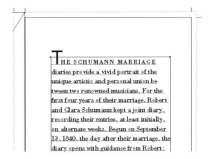

All of the elements placed into the layout

T HE SCHUMANN MARRIAGE diaries provide a vivid portrait of the unique artistic and personal union be tween two renowned musicians. For the first four years of their marriage, Robert and Clara Schumann kept a joint diary, recording their entries, at least initially, on alternate weeks. Begun on September 13, 1840, the day after their marriage, the diary opens with guidance from Robert:

Close-ups of an Area-Type object

ROBERT & CLARA SCHUMANN

Close-ups of Point-Type objects

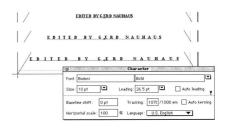

Tracking a line of Point Type with cursor-keys

Gallery: Pattie Belle Hastings, Bjørn Akselsen/Ice House Press & Design

When Ice House Press & Design (IHP&D) began to design labels for three different lines of oils and vinegars for an Italian client, they chose Illustrator as the production tool. Each line had to have a distinct identity, yet fit within the prescribed arched label shape. IHP&D found Illustrator ideal for designing such packaging labels, which combine graphics with highly modified type. IHP&D treated every block of type as a logo, manually kerning between each letter and word by clicking with the Type tool between letters and using the ← and → cursor-keys. (See the "Typographic Controls" tip on page 135.) IHP&D then manually selected and moved each graphic element and block of type until the spacing between the elements was just right. The ® mark, for instance, was individually created and placed as a separate element for each of the labels. Through this sort of meticulous manipulation, the type actually became graphical elements in a way not easily accomplished in a page layout program. For the Veritas line of organic olive oils, IHP&D chose to print in two PMS colors with gold foil for elegance (see Chapter 3 *for more on PMS colors). The Candoni line was designed for four PMS colors, while the third line (not pictured) was designed as a four-color process piece.*

Gallery: Javier Romero Design Group

Javier Romero Design Group converted the title in this illustration to outlines (Type: Create Outlines) and then manually distorted it. The resulting glowing effect, which the Design Group then applied to the type, can be used on any object—even regular, editable text objects. To replicate this effect, fill the top letter in a solid color, copy it and use Paste In Back (⌘-B) to place a copy of the letter behind the original. In the Paint Style palette, set the Fill for this copy to None, with a 5.5-pt, medium-colored stroke. Copy and Paste In Back this version and change the stroke weight to 7 points with a brighter color. Use Paste In Back again for an 11-pt, medium-colored stroke, and again for a dark, 16-pt stroke. (See Chapter 4 for making layers to help you isolate the versions.)

Gallery: Caryl Gorska / Max Seabaugh Associates

After commissioning Scott Baldwin to create a nutcracker illustration (he used Aldus FreeHand to re-create his linoleum cut), Caryl Gorska scanned a traditional, copyright-free Dover Publications typeface into the computer. She saved the scanned typeface as a PICT file (see page 80) and used the Pen tool to carefully trace the letters she needed. She then created the frame into which the type would be placed and, using the Selection tool, she "hand-set" the type by copying and pasting letter forms. Lastly, she fine-tuned the letter spacing, checking herself by printing myriad proofs—both actual size and greatly enlarged (increasing the percentage in Page Setup). Although her typeface, Newport Condensed, was available as a PostScript commercial font, instead of spending time and money tracking down and purchasing the font, Gorska preferred to spend the time typesetting the letters herself. "It keeps me in touch with the real letter forms and how they fit together, in a way that we often miss, just doing typesetting on the computer."

JAVIER ROMERO DESIGN GROUP

Gallery: Javier Romero Design Group

With a client as necessarily particular as Disney, Javier Romero needed the flexibility to create many design variations for children's clothing tags. And because the type needed to be fully integrated with the illustrations, Illustrator proved the most practical design tool. Of the dozens of designs that Romero presented, Disney selected as finals the designs shown in the photo above and to its right. Shown directly above are three of the comps, which include compositional elements contributing to the final design.

Masks & Special Effects

Advanced Techniques Chapter

8

Masks & Special Effects
Advanced Techniques

Introduction...

Masks ▶ Make
Release

Styling a masking object

In Illustrator 3.2, you could stroke or fill a mask because it was *behind* the objects it masked. Now, when you choose Object: Masks: Make, the *topmost* object automatically becomes the mask, and is restyled permanently with no fill and no stroke. However, to create the *illusion* that your mask is filled or stroked:

• Direct-select the mask and set the desired fill and / or stroke in the Paint Style palette.

• Then choose Filter: Create: Fill & Stroke for Mask to automatically generate a new filled object exactly behind the masked objects, and / or a new stroked object exactly on top of the masked objects.

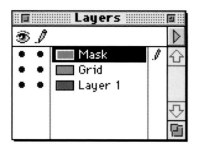

Ron Chan's Layers palette with a top Mask layer set to mask all lower layers

This Advanced Techniques chapter builds upon techniques and exercises covered in earlier chapters and combines techniques found in different chapters. With the masking effects in particular, the techniques will be easier to follow if you feel comfortable with layers (*Chapter 4*), as well as blends and gradients (*Chapter 5*), and are willing to tinker with the Pathfinder filters. Whenever necessary, I'll refer you to the proper chapter for more information on previously mentioned techniques.

Most techniques in this chapter make use of Illustrator's masks. Masks operate as stencils, or "clipping paths" that allow you to control which portions of objects will be visible. The simplest use of a mask is as a cropping tool. This defines the printable area of your page, cropping off from view or print any objects that extend beyond the boundary of the mask. Instead of using masks to define the printing boundary, many artists prefer simply to cover undesirable areas of an image with filled, white rectangles. But, the white rectangles end up being exported along with your image and creating false boundaries extending beyond the image. And, if you export an image with a masked boundary, the masks will actually trim off parts of the image beyond the mask's border.

Probably the best way to construct cropping boundaries is to create a "layer-mask." Working with a file that already has an image, choose Show Layers from the Window menu, make a new layer titled "Mask" and create your masking object in that layer (again, see *Chapter 4* for more info on layers). Then select the mask along with the backmost object in the stacking order that you wish to mask and choose Object: Masks: Make. Note that Illustrator masks any objects or layers between the mask and the backmost object you selected. You can move objects or entire layers above or below the mask, either to prevent them from being masked or to move them within the masked layers.

But masks can do much more than simply create boundaries for printing and exporting. Masks can also directly affect objects or groups of objects. In an object-mask, the mask and the objects are all in the same layer with the masking object on top. To *create* an object-mask, select all the objects including the top object which will become the mask, and choose Object: Masks: Make. If you accidentally select objects on layers other than the one you want to mask, then all other objects in between the mask and the chosen object will also be masked. To correct this problem, use Shift-Direct-select on any objects that were inadvertently masked to deselect them, then group (⌘-G) the mask with the desired objects. Grouping will place all masked objects on the same layer as the mask and restrict the masking effect to those objects within the grouping.

Masks were once the only way to achieve certain effects that you can now accomplish using features introduced in Illustrator 5. For example, you can now use gradients to make transitions within complex objects both linearly and radially (see *Chapter 5* for more on blends and gradients), although you'll see throughout this chapter many shaped blends that can't yet be created with gradients. Also, Pathfinder filters can now actually crop off unwanted parts of objects that at one time required masking (see *Chapter 6*); however, these filters irrevocably alter the shapes of objects, greatly limiting your ability to make changes at a later time.

Illustrator's masking feature provides an extraordinary amount of control over what portions of objects, blends or images are visible. Masks let you easily adjust both the contour of the masking object and the contents of objects being masked, through use of the Direct-Select tool to edit paths and the Group-select tool to isolate objects. To insert additional objects into a mask, cut or copy them, select an object within the mask and use Paste In Front or Back (⌘-F or ⌘-B) to place the copied object into the mask.

Finding masks

Although layer-masks (see page opposite) aren't always detectable, deselecting all objects first and choosing Select: Select Masks filter should help you find most masks.

Grouping masks

Group an object-mask with its objects (⌘-G) for easy reselecting. However, if you group a layer-mask with its objects, it will convert to an object-mask, with all objects moving to the mask's layer (see text at left).

Figuring out if it's a mask

If you're not sure whether a current selection contains a mask, or is being masked, choose Object: Attributes (⌘-Control-A). Or, look to see if the Release toggle is enabled under Object: Masks— indicating that a mask is affecting the current selection.

Memory-hogging masks

Masks require a lot of memory. Too many masks, or complex masking paths, may prevent you from printing. To test if a specific mask is a problem, select it along with its masked objects, temporarily hide (⌘-3) all of them and see if printing is easier.
IMPORTANT: *Hiding only the mask will not affect the masked objects.*

Colorful Masking

Fitting Blends into Custom Shapes

Advanced Technique

Overview: *Create a complex blend; mask it with a custom masking object; create a second mask-and-blend combination; make a two-object mask using compound paths.*

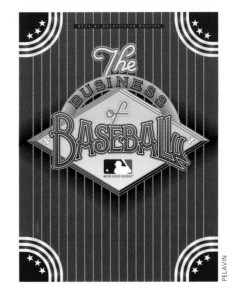

The best way to learn how to mask is to make some masked blends. With Laurie Grace's pencils, you'll learn how to mask complex blends to fit into custom shapes. And with the patriotic corners of Danny Pelavin's baseball illustration, you'll learn how to mask one blend into two different objects by using compound paths.

The gradient for a pencil body

1 Creating the basic elements not requiring masking. Create your basic objects. For her pencils, Grace created the long barrel of the pencil with a gradient fill.

Creating objects and blending them in pairs, then creating an object to use as a mask

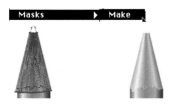

Selecting the blends with an overlying object designed as a mask; the objects masked

2 Creating the first mask-and-blend combination. To prepare a mask for the pencils, create a closed object outlining the shaved wooden ridges and the pencil tip, and choose Lock (⌘-1). To ensure that your blend will fill the mask completely as you create the basic objects for the blend, make sure that each object extends beyond the mask. Then select and blend each pair of adjacent objects (see *Chapter 5*). Grace created the slanted outside objects first, and the center object last so the blends would build from back to front towards the center. Unlock (⌘-2) your pencil-tip object, bring it to the front (⌘-=), select the blends with the mask, and choose Object: Masks: Make. Finally, group (⌘-G) the mask and the blend together.

3 Preparing the next masking objects and mask. Select and copy your mask, then select and lock the mask with the masked objects to keep from accidentally selecting any of them as you continue to work. Next, use Paste In Front (⌘-F) to paste a copy of your previous mask on top, and make any adjustments necessary to prepare this object as the next mask. Grace cut and reshaped a copy of the full pencil-tip mask until it correctly fit the colored lead at the top. Finally, you'll want to hide (⌘-3) this new mask-to-be until you've completed a new set of blends.

Completed objects selected and locked, then a copy of the last mask made into a new mask

4 Creating a new mask that overlies the first. Create and blend new pairs of objects as you did for the previous mask. When your blends are complete, show (⌘-4) your hidden masking object and choose Arrange: Bring To Front (⌘-=) to place the mask on top of these latest blends. Then select the colored-tip blends with this top object, choose Object: Masks: Make and, as before, group them (⌘-G) together for easy reselection. Finally, unlock the first blends (⌘-2), select the entire piece and group (⌘-G) it all together.

New objects before and after blending, and after being masked

5 Making a mask from a compound path. Create a blend to be masked by two objects. As Pelavin did for his patriotic corners, start with a circle as a template. In Artwork mode, use the Pen tool with the Shift key to draw a straight line from the circle's center point to its bottom edge. With the Rotate tool, Option-click on the circle center to specify an 11.25° rotation and click Copy. Then press ⌘-D seven times to repeat the rotated copy a full quarter of a circle. Recolor every other line and blend from one to the next as above. Next, create two paths for a mask (Pelavin cut and joined quarters of concentric circles) and choose Object: Compound Paths: Make. Place the compound paths on top of the blends, select them all and choose Object: Masks: Make to see your blend show through both compound paths. Pelavin recolored a copy of the red blend with a range of whites, masked the white blend with a larger arc, and placed it behind the reds. ◠

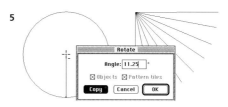

Rotating a copy of a line about a circle's center 11.25°, then using ⌘-D to transform 7 times

Coloring every other line and blending in pairs

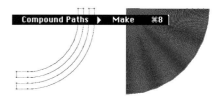

Compounding paths and getting ready to mask

Blends masked by compounds and a final corner (shown here also with a masked white blend)

Offsetting Colors
Using Masks to Create Relief & Shadows

Advanced Technique

Overview: *Create a basic object stroked in white; offset a copy in a medium tone; copy and Paste In Front light and dark copies and mask them; Paste In Front the final color.*

Creating the basic three positions and colors

Making highlight, shadow and masking-object

Filling with no stroke or fill and creating the mask

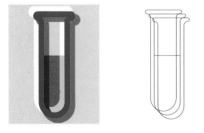

The final tube in Preview and Artwork modes

Creating the illusion of relief is a result of both finding the right colors and placing the objects in the correct relationship to each other. For a *Time* magazine article, "The Chemistry of Love," Joe Lertola relied solely on a limited palette, objects offset in three positions and Illustrator's masking feature to create this license plate.

1 Creating a simple object stroked in white, then offsetting copies. Set the ruler units to points (see Tip on page 20). Select any object using the Paint Style palette, set it to a 2.5-pt white stroke with no fill. Hold down the Option key and drag a copy down and to the right 2.5 points, or Option-click on the Selection tool to open the Move dialog box, specify a 2.5 Horizontal and –2.5 Vertical move and click Copy. Style this copy in a medium blue-gray. Using the same technique, make another copy halfway between the objects (–1.25-pt horizontal and 1.25 vertical), remove the stroke and give it a fill of red. For the tubes, Lertola cut this red, topmost object so it appears half-filled (see page 52 and *Chapter 6* for different approaches to cutting an object).

2 Making the inner shadow and highlight. Copy the white object, deselect, choose Edit: Paste In Front (⌘-F) and change the stroke to a light tint of the red. Then copy the blue-gray object, deselect, Paste In Front and style it with a dark burgundy stroke. Copy the red-filled object, deselect, and Paste In Front, styling this copy with no stroke or fill. Select this last copy, the original red object, the light tint and the dark shadow, and choose Object: Masks: Make. Offset a final copy of the full object's outline on top, in the halfway position, and set a blue, 1.8-pt stroke.

TUTTLE

Gallery: Jean Tuttle

In this Santa Barbara Film Festival image, Jean Tuttle created the wavy film sprockets by first setting the Constrain-angle to 45° (which rotates anchor points 45° off-center) and making a circle. From the center of this circle, she made a smaller, concentric circle by Option-Shift-dragging with the Oval tool. Selecting both circles, Tuttle used the Blend tool to create a third circle between them. Next, selecting the smallest circle, Tuttle Option-clicked with the Rotate tool on the lower right anchor point to rotate 180° and clicked Copy. From the center point of this copied circle, she made two smaller, concentric circles, dragging until they "snapped" to the next arc of the larger circle. She Direct-select marqueed the points on the circles above and below the wave shape and deleted, then selected and joined (⌘-J) each pair of overlapping anchor points. Tuttle next Option-Shift-dragged sideways a copy of the wave until it snapped into position so she could join it to the first. She dragged copies of the long wave downward and joined them to form both a wide black ribbon and a thinner, white path. After making two white rectangles and blending them to form regular strips across, Tuttle masked them with the thin wave path. She also recolored copies of the blended rectangles and used them elsewhere, such as the water (bottom of image) in which turquoise bars overlap a gradient rectangle made from tints of the same turquoise color.

Contouring Masks

Using Masks to Control Realistic Tonality

Advanced Technique

Overview: *Create the full outline for your image; copy an object representing a surface; create a blend and mask it with a copy of the surface outline pasted in front.*

1

Initial printer in Artwork mode (notice that objects don't overlap)

The top objects before blending

The top blended and selected with top object before masking

The top masked

There are a number of reasons why you should learn how to replicate the gradient effect (see *Chapter 5*) using blends and masks. First, blends which are made up of a limited number of steps can print more quickly than gradients. Second, gradients that print smoothly won't necessarily look good for on-screen presentations. Finally, by learning this technique, you'll understand how to edit complex images saved in formats prior to Illustrator 5.

Since Andrea Kelley knows that her renderings for Apple Computer are often printed in miniature (less than 1" tall) or viewed on computer monitors, she controls how the images will be displayed on the monitor, while reducing the printing time for her miniatures. Kelley does this by using blends and masked blends instead of gradients. For blends within straight-sided objects, Kelley removes unnecessary paths to keep the blends clean in Artwork mode (see page 114). For rounded shapes, Kelley uses copies of an object's contour to mask her blends.

1 After creation of a full image outline, creating and masking blends. Create an outline version of your image, constructing each surface you'd like to mask out of one closed object (see page 122 for one way to create separate enclosed objects). Decide which surface you'd like to mask first, select the corresponding object and copy it, then choose Edit: Select All (⌘-A). Now Lock (⌘-1) all the selected objects. Create a blend that extends beyond the surface parameters, then use Paste In Front to paste the copy of your surface (your new mask) on top. Select the blend along with the top object and choose Object: Masks: Make. Then group (⌘-G) the mask with its blend.

To access the other objects in your illustration, choose Unlock (⌘-2). Then continue to follow the above steps for each surface requiring a different tonality or color. As you work, make sure to lock objects you don't want to select accidentally, and to group masks with their objects as soon as they're made. You may wish to group related objects further for easy reselection—for example, all of the objects forming the top of the printer.

Simplify your tasks by making and using custom layers to isolate objects as you work (see *Chapter 4* for details on layers). Try, for instance, pasting the next object you intend to use as a mask into a new, upper layer labeled "red." After you create the mask, grouping it with the masked objects will automatically move the masked objects into the upper red layer. By having this red layer, you'll be able to identify instantly and lock or hide all previously masked objects as you select the next surface to prepare it for masking. And there's no need to stop at one extra layer. Whenever you find it difficult to isolate particular elements, create a new layer (assigning it a new selection color) and move the appropriate objects to the layer by dragging the colored dots at the right of the current layer to the new layer (see last Tip on page 88).

2 Creating details through careful observation. Kelley uses 100% blacks and whites with only occasional small, thin lines as highlight or shadow accents. Copy and use Paste In Front on paths, or parts of paths, and restyle them as accents (see pages 50 and 114 for suggestions). ✐

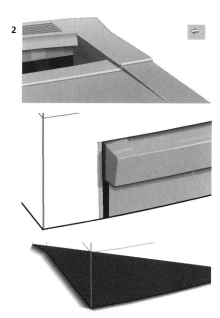

Details of the masked printer blends

The final printer in Artwork mode

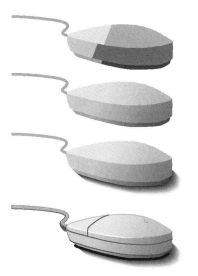

The mouse's mask-and-blend progression

Magically transform gradients into masked blends

To transform gradients into masked blends, save a copy of the file in Illustrator 3 format; upon reopening, gradients will be replaced by masked blends! —*Tip by AK*

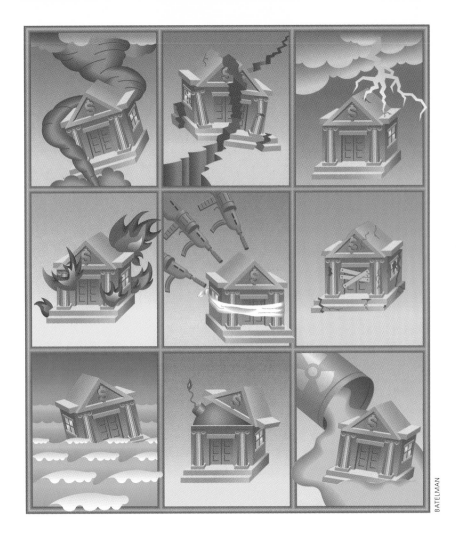

BATELMAN

Gallery: Kenneth Batelman

Kenneth Batelman used masks to fit blends into contoured shapes all through-out this "Banking Disaster" illustration. Shown directly above are the stages of creating the flames, from making pure blends, to masking with a flame shape, to layering flames upon flames. Batelman used a similar technique to fit blends within a poured shape for the glowing, radioactive slime, and to shape the tornado funnel. He also used masks to create splits in the earthquake image (each split contains an entire bank, masked to show only the desired portion), and in the clouds and waves.

MORRIS / SAN FRANCISCO EXAMINER

Gallery: Christopher Morris / *San Francisco Examiner*

Christopher Morris created "Mafia Chef" for a San Francisco Examiner *story about a Mafia member who, after entering the Federal Witness Protection Program, wrote a cookbook and then went out on tour promoting it, only giving interviews in clandestine hotel rooms. To create this darkly satirical illustration, Morris constructed blends that fit roughly into compositional outlines that he had drawn with the Pen tool. He then used his compositional outlines as masks to fit the rough blends snugly into these contours. Shown directly above, from left to right is the chef, constructed only of blends (notice that the blends stick out in various places), next with the contouring masks in place, and then, after being masked. Also shown is the corner with the steaming pot before and after masks were applied.*

Reflective Masks

Super-Realistic Reflection

Advanced Technique

Overview: *Move a copy of a blend area; if you're using type, convert it to outlines; skew and adjust it to the right shape; use filters to make an offset; recolor and remask blends; move blend back into position.*

1

A blended area selected and a copy moved off the image area (using ⌘-Shift-Option and cursor-keys set to 1.5" increments); and type converted to outlines

2

Skewing outlined type, then adjusting and coloring it to fit the blend contour

Creating reflections for an "outline" by copying the type, then stroking and filtering it using Objects: Outline Path and Pathfinder: Unite

Two techniques in earlier chapters demonstrated how Thomas•Bradley Illustration & Design (T•BI&D) used Pathfinder filters to generate its basic objects for blending (page 122), and how the blends themselves are formed (page 112). This technique focuses on replicating contouring blends to create reflectivity and surface variation.

1 **Replicating an area of your image for placing new details.** This process can be used to create color or surface variations, but we'll use the application of type detailing as a demonstration. After you've outlined your image and filled it with contouring blends, choose an area for detailing. With the Shift key, use the Selection and Group-selection tools to select all blends and originating objects for the blends that exist in the area. Open up Preferences and set the Cursor-key distance to 1.5". With the ⌘-Shift-Option keys down, press the → key and notice that a copy of the selected blends moves 1.5" to the right! Let go of the ⌘-Shift-Option keys and continue to move the blends until they are in a blank area of your image. Type a letter, word or number on top of the moved blend (see *Chapter 7* for more on type), then click on a selection tool to select it as an *object* (instead of as editable type) and choose Type: Create Outlines.

2 **Reshaping type to fit your blended contours and creating an offset.** Working from templates, references, or just your artistic eye, use the Rotate, Scale and Skew tools with Direct-selection to adjust various anchor points until the type fits the contour. For the type on the racecar, T•BI&D skewed the letters (by clicking first in the center

of a baseline, grabbing above right, and Shift-dragging to the right), then Direct-selected individual points and groups of points, moving them into the visually correct positions.

To create the outlining effect, first copy a solid-filled version, then stroke your selection in the desired weight and color. Choose Filter: Objects: Outline Path, and while it's still selected, choose Filter: Pathfinder: Unite.

3 Pasting the original back on top, designing new colors for copies of the older blends and masking the new versions. First, Paste In Front (⌘-F) the original, unstroked type element. With the Group-selection tool, click twice on one object in a blend to select the entire group of blended objects, write down how many steps there are in the blend (so you can replicate it later in other colors), and delete, leaving the original two source objects. Repeat for other blends overlapping the area you're detailing. Select and lock (⌘-1) blends or objects that won't fall within the detail, but that you want to keep for reference. Copy and Paste In Front (⌘-F) each of the source objects for new blends and recolor them for your detailing. Reblend each pair of source objects using the same number of steps as you did originally, grouping (⌘-G) these objects with their blends as you go. T·BI&D recolored the car blends for the red "3," then added a tear-shaped blend for more detail. Select and copy (in Artwork mode if necessary) the original "3," use Paste In Front (⌘-F), press the Shift key to add the grouped new blends to the selection, then choose Object: Masks: Make. Group (⌘-G) and hide (⌘-3) these finished masked objects and repeat for any additional highlights and shadows. Show All (⌘-4) when these masks are complete, group all the masks together (⌘-G) and use the cursor-keys to snap this group of reflective details into position. T·BI&D created one more version of the "3" for a dark offset. For areas requiring more reflections, they constructed even more masks upon masks, as well as occasionally applying compound-masks (see page 154). ◠

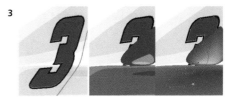

Re-creating blends in new colors and preparing to mask them with a copy of the "3" on top

With the red, reflective blends masked, creating a darker, offset "3"

The dark "3" and the entire group of objects complete, before and after being moved back into position with cursor-keys

Other elements require more stages of blending (see page 154 for compounding multiple objects, like type elements, to apply as a single mask)

Glowing Starshine

Blending Custom Colors to Form a Glow

Advanced Technique

Overview: *Create a custom color for the background and the basic object; scale a copy of the object; make object adjustments and blend a glow.*

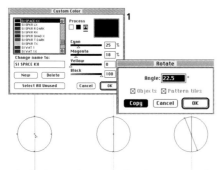

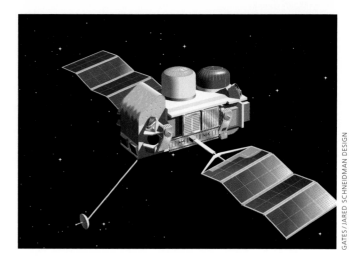

GATES/JARED SCHNEIDMAN DESIGN

The background custom color; dragging a guide to the center of a circle, drawing a center line and rotating a copy of the line

After pressing ⌘-D six times, making guides and adding anchor points at guide intersections

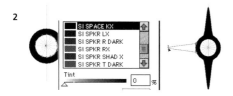

After Shift-Option scaling the circle smaller and changing the center to 0% tint; Direct-selecting and moving top, bottom and side points outward

Before and after a 12-step blend

Illumination is the key to creating a realistic nighttime sky. This variation on a technique by Guilbert Gates and Jared Schneidman Design (JSD) will help you create glowing lights, not just stars, simply and directly.

1 Creating a custom color and the basic object. Create a background rectangle filled with a dark, custom color (see *Chapter 3*). JSD's background was 25% cyan, 18% magenta and 100% black. In Artwork mode, make a circle, then drag a guideline from the ruler until it "snaps" to the circle's center (see Tip on page 7). With the Pen tool, click on an edge of the circle where the guide intersects, hold down Shift and click on the other edge. Select this line, double-click the Rotate tool, specify 22.5° and click Copy. Type ⌘-D to repeat the rotate/copy six times, then select only the lines and type ⌘-5 to make them guides. Use the Add-anchor-point tool to add eight points, one on each side of the circle's original points at guide intersections.

2 Creating the glow. With the circle selected, use the Scale tool to make a smaller copy of the circle (hold the Shift and Option keys) and specify a 0% tint fill in the Paint Style palette. Direct-select the top point and Shift-drag it outward. Repeat with the bottom and two side points. With the Blend tool, click on corresponding selected points from each circle and specify 12 steps. ✑

Gallery: Bill Snebold

To create this juggling clown, Bill Snebold first traced a scanned sketch (see Chapter 4*) of the left side of the clown with the Pen tool, then made a flipped copy for the right side using the Reflect tool. Snebold traced the apple from a Polaroid photo and carefully created blends throughout (see* Chapter 5*). For the glowing apples, he made a full red apple using blends, then drew subsections of the apple to use as masks. For each color on the apple, he reconfigured the blend colors of the entire apple (see page 162), placed the appropriate subsection path on top and chose Object: Masks: Make. The glows result specifically from blending sections of the apple contour filled with white to the overlapping background color. Where the apple overlapped the face, Snebold had to create approximately 20 blends, many of them masked individually.*

Gallery: K. Daniel Clark

To create this cut-away for Windows *magazine, K. Daniel Clark began with a variation of the perspective lines covered on page 96. With the Pen tool, Clark drew three lines: a horizon line and two vanishing-point lines (one left and one right). He didn't make these lines into Illustrator guides, but kept them as paths for easy adjustability and for drawing all parallel sides. By grabbing the free anchor point (not the vanishing point), Clark could pull it to the next location where he needed it. To create the cut-away illusion, he first filled the scanner "box" with separate objects representing the various parts (using the perspective lines as guides). Then he created objects to form the top, curved-page shadow, leaving part of the objects below exposed. For finishing touches, Clark gave the walls "some thickness" by drawing a top edge, created shadows and highlights and placed additional details within the scanner. He deleted the perspective lines before saving a final version to send to the client.*

Gallery: Andrea Kelley

For a series of promotional baseball cards produced for Symantec Corporation, Andrea Kelley developed a system to distort the dozens of logos and pictures needing to be placed onto boxes in an identical turned-angle perspective. Kelley first drew a box using the Pen tool, then grouped (⌘-G) and scaled her first logo to a rectangle the size of the angled placeholder on the box (see Chapter 2 and the Tip "Scaling images to an exact size" on page 13 for scaling help). Because the turned face was thinner than a box front, she double-clicked on the Scale tool to specify 85% horizontal (100% vertical) scaling. She dragged the logo from the upper left corner until it snapped to the upper left corner of the turned face. With the Rotate tool, Kelley then clicked on the upper left point again, grabbed the upper right corner and swung it up until it aligned with the top of the box. Next, with the Skew tool, she clicked once more on the upper left corner of the face, grabbed the lower right corner and, holding the Shift key, swung it down until that line aligned with the spine of the box. After moving the logo into alignment with the left corner of the spine and top of the box, she aligned the lower right corner to the box by first clicking Reset and moving the lower right corner up the minimum amount, applying Filter: Free Distort twice. Finally, she held the Option key and chose Filter: Distort: Free Distort again to reset, then slid the right corner to the left a minimal amount.

Painterly Effects

From Gradient Lighting to Painterly Trees

Advanced Technique

Overview: *Create an illustration in full outline; use filters and manual cut and join tools to separate sections and soften edges containing gradients.*

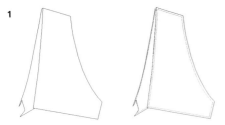

Artwork view of original roof outline and after the SCT Inset Path filter from the **Wow!** disk

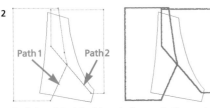

Path 1 and Path 2 objects before and after applying the Roughen filter

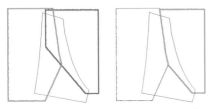

A copy of Path 1 selected with Path 2, then after the Minus Front filter

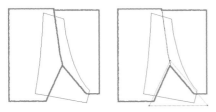

Copies of Path 1 and Path 2, and after the paths have been united, with a third path added

Some circumstances require more than just filling each object with a gradient fill (see *Chapter 5*). Clarke Tate's night rendering of Mann's Chinese Theater for *USA Today* contains many examples of layering gradients upon gradients, and of using filters to transform Illustrator's normally hard-edged look into a more painterly effect.

1 Making inset subsections of architectural objects and filling them with different gradients. With the Pen tool, create detailed outlines of your image, using enlarged templates if necessary (Tate starts with 400% enlarged templates, *Chapter 4*). Since you'll be filling with gradients, make your outlines completely closed paths. Select a simple object, such as a roof, and create an inset copy of it using the SCT Inset Path filter from the *Wow!* disk (make sure to place this filter into the Plug-ins folder and restart Illustrator). Choose Filter: Objects: SCT Inset Path, and specify 6 points. If you are working on a smaller scale, you might prefer a smaller inset.

2 Creating roughened divisions to diminish contrast between gradients. Start by selecting the roof inset and hiding (Option-⌘-3) everything else. You're going to split the roof into four pie-shaped sections so you can vary the gradients within the roof. With the Pen tool, draw closed Path 1, which will surround the entire left side of the roof, bisecting two-thirds of the roof vertically and angling back toward the left so that it forms the left side of a "peace-sign." For closed Path 2, surround the entire right side of the roof, creating the right side of the peace-sign and overlapping Path 1.

Select both paths, choose Filter: Distort: Roughen and specify a 15% size and 30 segments with the Jagged option. Make a new layer (see *Chapter 4*) and place a copy of Path 1 on that layer by selecting Path 1 and Option-dragging its dot in the Layers palette into the new layer. Shift-select Path 2 as well and choose Filter: Pathfinder: Minus Front to cut the copy of Path 1 from Path 2.

3 Creating the bottom of the roof sections. Make a new layer, select Paths 1 and 2 and place copies of these paths in the new layer. With the paths still selected, choose Filter: Pathfinder: Unite. Next, on a lower layer, create a triangle that extends beyond the bottom of the roof and overlaps Path 1 and Path 2. Then Shift-select the united path on top, and again, choose the Minus Front Pathfinder filter to cut the united path from the triangle.

Draw a last triangle surrounding the right half of the bottom section, choose Filter: Distort: Roughen and use the same settings as before. Now drag a copy of the bottom section to another layer, Shift-select the newest triangle and choose the Pathfinder: Intersect filter.

To fit all these objects within the original roof inset, drag a copy of the roof inset to the top layer. Shift-select

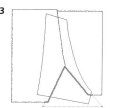
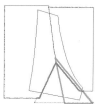

3

After the Minus Front filter, and before using Intersect on the last roughened shape

Before and after the Crop filter

4

The roof after being cut into sections and filled with custom gradients, and customized with the Gradient-fill tool

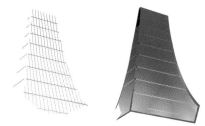

Outlining paths to fill them with gradients

The final roof in Artwork and Preview

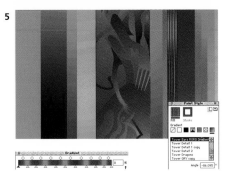

5

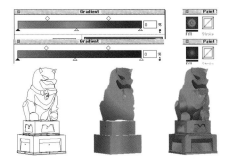

A detail of the tower and one of the gradients, shown in both the Gradient and Paint palettes

The main and "recessed" gradients for the lion, shown in Artwork mode, then progressively filled with gradients

Progressive stages of theater detail and the taxi-cab gradient

all four sections of this copy, set a temporary fill style and choose Filter: Pathfinder: Crop.

4 Designing the roof lighting effects. To represent different lighting conditions that affect a roof surface, design some custom gradients (see *Chapter 5*). Tate used two basic color ranges for the roof: a bright, wide-ranging, yellow-to-red radial, and a dark, linear gradient in a range of red-browns. Apply darker gradient to the back objects, with brighter gradients for the front objects. Use the Gradient-fill tool to customize the fill direction in each section (page 108), then group (⌘-G) the roof elements.

Next, with the Pen tool, create stroked lines following the vertical slope of the roof and group them. Using a thicker stroke, create tiling lines that follow the horizontal slope of the roof and group them. Finally, select both the horizontal and vertical lines (with the Selection tool) and choose Filter: Objects: Outline Path to convert these strokes to filled paths. Now fill each group of "lines" with gradients, unifying them with the Gradient-fill tool.

5 Filling and customizing overlapping objects with multicolored gradients. The more detail you'd like in your image, the more overlapping objects you'll need to create. Again, because you'll be filling these details with gradients, make sure to create closed objects. As you work, group (⌘-G) related objects together for easy reselection.

Design new gradients for different ranges of light and surface in other parts of the theater. Since you've grouped related objects together, Direct-select individual objects to fill each with a gradient. As with the roof, use the Gradient-fill tool to customize each fill (again, see page 108). For his tower wall, Tate created elaborate multicolored gradients. For the lion, he used two radial gradients: the primary gradient covered a wide color and value range, while the shadow gradient remained dark in tone.

6 Creating the front canopy for a painterly tree. Make the basic object for your tree canopy, copy it, and lock

(⌘-1) it. Paste In Front (⌘-F) the copied canopy and apply the following filters, one after the other: Add Anchor Points (twice), Distort: Roughen (specifying a 5% size, a detail of 10 segments and the Jagged option) and Stylize: Round Corners at the default setting.

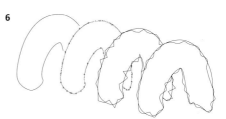

The original canopy and after Add-anchor-points, Roughen and Round Corners filters

7 Creating the back canopy and "holes" for branches to show through. Unlock (⌘-2) the original, undistorted canopy and, while it's selected, apply the Objects: Add Anchor Points filter three times, then Distort: Roughen (specifying 5%, 10 segments and Rounded). Temporarily fill each shape with different solid colors so you can distinguish them in Preview mode. Make a new, irregularly shaped object to use as a hole in the front canopy. Select this new object with the front canopy and choose Filter: Pathfinder: Minus Front. Then create another object to use as a hole in the back canopy, of roughly the same size and location, but shaped differently enough so you can see parts of the back object while still seeing through to your background. Select this object with the back canopy and choose Minus Front from the top of the Filter list.

Roughening the back and cutting holes

8 Creating the trunk and branches. Set your Paint Style palette with a 4-pt stroke weight and no fill, and draw a basic trunk with the Pen tool. For branches, create paths of progressively smaller line weights as you move up the tree, then group the branches with the trunk and transform these lines into filled objects with Filter: Objects: Outline Path. Now taper the objects of the trunk and branches, and fill each portion of the tree with custom radial gradients by using the Gradient-fill tool.

Adjusting outlined paths for trunk and branches

9 Creating the leaves. For the finishing foliage, lock (⌘-1) the tree and create random-sized, light-colored circles with the Oval tool. Select all the circles, group them and apply the Distort: Roughen filter (specifying 60%, 10 segments and Rounded). Direct-select to refill individual leaves. ◡

Making leaves from filtered circles

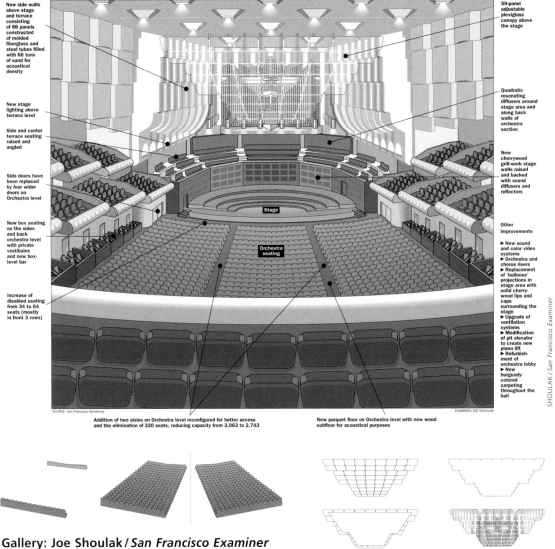

New side walls above stage and terrace consisting of 88 panels constructed of molded fiberglass and steel tubes filled with 66 tons of sand for acoustical density

New stage lighting above terrace level

Side and center terrace seating raised and angled

Side doors have been replaced by four wider doors on Orchestra level

New box seating on the sides and back orchestra level with private vestibules and new box-level bar

Increase of disabled seating from 34 to 64 seats (mostly in front 3 rows)

59-panel adjustable plexiglass canopy above the stage

Quadratic resonating diffusers around stage area and along back walls of orchestra section

New cherrywood grill-work stage walls raised and backed with sound diffusers and reflectors

Other improvements

► New sound and color video systems
► Orchestra and chorus risers
► Replacement of 'bullnose' projections in stage area with solid cherrywood lips and caps surrounding the stage
► Upgrade of ventilation systems
► Modification of pit elevator to create new piano lift
► Refurbishment of orchestra lobby
► New burgundy-colored carpeting throughout the hall

Stage

Orchestra seating

SOURCE: San Francisco Symphony

EXAMINER/JOE SHOULAK

Addition of two aisles on Orchestra level reconfigured for better access and the elimination of 320 seats, reducing capacity from 3,063 to 2,743

New parquet floor on Orchestra level with new wood subfloor for acoustical purposes

SHOULAK / *San Francisco Examiner*

Gallery: Joe Shoulak / *San Francisco Examiner*

For this illustration detailing the renovation of Davies Symphony Hall, Joe Shoulak drew the first row of seats, then duplicated, moved, darkened, rotated and skewed it. He then blended the two rows using 18 steps. Shoulak next selected and grouped the left seats and, with the Reflect tool, he Option-clicked to the right of the seats to specify a reflection along the vertical axis, and clicked Copy. For the Plexiglass canopy, he skewed, scaled, and reflected rounded rectangles. Shoulak united a copy of the rectangles into one object (by placing an overlapping solid object with the rectangles, and choosing Pathfinder: Unite). He copied the objects that he wished to have appear through the canopy, moved them into a new document (in perfect registration) using Paste In Front, and desaturated the colors (Filter: Colors: Desaturate). Shoulak pasted the united canopy on top of the desaturated panels and masked with it. He stroked the rectangles white (no fill) and pasted them on top of the masked panels. Then he grouped and copied the entire Plexiglass section and used Paste In Front to bring it back on top of the main image.

Illustrator & Other Programs

9

Illustrator & Other Programs

Introduction...

Opening placed EPS images

From Illustrator, Option-double-click on a placed EPS image to open that file in its "native application"—as long as you have enough memory available to run both programs (see Tip on page 3).

Resizing and line weight

In Illustrator, if you double-click the Scale tool, you can resize your selection with or without altering line weights (see page 13):

- To scale a selection while also scaling line weights, make sure to enable "Scale line weight."
- To scale a selection while maintaining your line weights, disable "Scale line weight."
- To decrease only line weights (let's say, 50%) without scaling objects, first scale the selection (200%) with "Scale line weight" disabled. Then scale (50%) with "Scale line weight" enabled. Reverse to increase line weights.

STEUER

Since this entire book is dedicated to showing you Adobe Illustrator, you can by now begin to see the folly in attempting to present step-by-step instructions in any real depth for working with other programs—each program is probably deserving of a volume in itself. So instead, this chapter will present a range of work in Gallery format, showing Illustrator in combination with other frequently used programs. This chapter should whet your appetite for delving into the world of software juggling, as well as broadening your vision of how to use Adobe Illustrator.

Most people know that Illustrator images can be placed into layout programs (page 193), but few know that layout programs can be reworked in Illustrator (page 194).

One of the most compelling reasons to use Illustrator is that you can resize Illustrator images without sacrificing detail. Once an image is properly sized, you can "rasterize" it (transform it into a bitmapped format made of pixels) while preserving an incredible amount of the detail (see page 176 for how to do this in Photoshop, and Galleries throughout the chapter). This makes Illustrator ideal for images that need to be scaled to extremes, from billboards to multimedia presentations (pages 191–192).

Photoshop represents probably the easiest way to rasterize your Illustrator objects—turning them into smooth, "antialiased" (non-jaggy) bitmapped images. Because Adobe Systems develops both Illustrator and Photoshop, the interrelationship is, well, almost symbiotic. And, since so many people have Photoshop, this chapter includes a step-by-step technique for bringing Illustrator images into Photoshop, as demonstrated by renowned artist and author Bert Monroy.

Two other Adobe programs also popular with Illustrator users are Dimensions and Streamline. Dimensions allows you to create 3D-looking Illustrator files or to distort your Illustrator files in 3D space (pages 190–191). Streamline is a program for converting bitmapped images (painted or scanned) into Illustrator files. Although Streamline was apparently developed to be a sophisticated auto-tracing tool for scanned line art (logos, for example), most Illustrator artists find they get better results tracing line art by hand with the Pen tool. (Illustrator's Auto-trace tool provides even less control, but if you want to experiment, learn about it in the *User Guide*.) However, Streamline can be pushed far beyond its role as a production tracing aid. A number of artists are using Streamline creatively to translate scanned drawings or photos into Illustrator images that look completely different from what you usually think of as being created in Illustrator (pages 182–184).

In addition to being able to bring Illustrator *objects* into other programs, you can import and export Illustrator *paths* (as they appear in Artwork mode). Painter lets you import Illustrator paths as "friskets," or stencils, which allow you to isolate regions of your image to apply painting and other effects selectively (page 186). Photoshop 3.0 allows you to copy and paste paths, export paths to Illustrator, or create Illustrator-like paths within Photoshop itself. In Photoshop, paths can define selection areas for isolating areas of your image, or can be used to define "clipping paths" (pages 176–177, 184, 188, and Tip on this page, top right).

Lastly, you can import Illustrator paths as outlines and extrusion paths into 3D programs, so you can transform these paths into 3D objects. Unlike Dimensions, which creates Illustrator objects that only look as if they are 3D, true 3D programs maintain their three-dimensional characteristics until you decide to "render" an image as an antialiased bitmap. Strata's StudioPro (page 189), and RayDream Designer (pages 187–188) are two 3D programs you can use in combination with Illustrator. Be aware that each 3D program sports a unique interface, and that you're likely to feel more comfortable in some environments than others. Try to see demos of each 3D program, and plan to get at least some initial training in the program that you choose.

Illustrator for "clipping paths"

Just as you can use masks in Illustrator to define irregularly shaped boundaries for your objects, or for the entire image (see *Chapter 8*), a number of programs allow you to save in certain formats that use Illustrator paths to create a "clipping path," which defines the boundaries of the image when placed in other programs. Shown below is Photoshop's method.

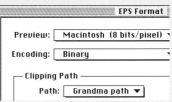

Creating and defining a clipping path in Photoshop 3.0, then applying the clipping path to the image when saving in EPS format (see page 108 to see this "clipped" image placed into Illustrator)

Drag-and-Drop?

If you have the Macintosh Drag and Drop Extension (it's automatically installed with System 7.5 and up) then you can drag and drop some selections between Illustrator and Photoshop—bypassing the need to Copy and Paste. See ⑥ for more about the benefits and limitations of drag and drop.

Sketching Tools

Illustrator as a Primary Drawing Tool

Illustrator with Photoshop

Overview: *Create your details in Illustrator; place Illustrator images into Photoshop at the right size; render and finish in Photoshop.*

1

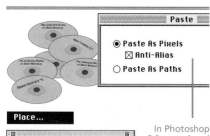

In Photoshop 3.0, put placed and pasted images into a separate layer for maximum flexibility

Three ways Illustrator images can be brought into Photoshop: opening, pasting and placing

©Bert Monroy '92

MONROY

With a Powerbook portable Macintosh, Bert Monroy meets with his clients to sketch ideas directly in Adobe Illustrator. Back in his studio, Monroy transforms these sketches into intricately detailed illustrations, which he then scales to the desired size, without sacrificing any of the detail. Monroy constructs his Illustrator images in flat colors and then brings them into Photoshop, where he can rework them into scenes rich in texture, light, shadow and volume.

1 Bringing detailed Illustrator images into Photoshop. There are a number of ways for you to bring Illustrator images into Photoshop. First, from within Photoshop, choose File: Open and select an Illustrator file. Specify the size and resolution at which you plan to rasterize (turn into a bitmap) the image. Experiment with the results of changing the options. Second, copy the image in

Illustrator, and paste directly into Photoshop, choosing to paste "as pixels." Pasting "as paths" (new in Photoshop 3.0) imports paths to use in defining selections, or to serve as "clipping paths" for saving Photoshop files with nonrectangular boundaries. Third, if you have an open image, you can choose the File: Place command. With the Place command, you can visually resize your Illustrator image before it's rendered (see page 25). If you have Photoshop 3.0 (and I *highly* recommend it), place or paste Illustrator files into separate layers so you can easily alter and move them in relation to the rest of the image.

2 Measuring in Photoshop and resizing in Illustrator.

One of the greatest strengths of bringing Illustrator images into Photoshop is that you can render the maximum amount of detail at any resolution. If you resize (smaller or larger) a rendered Illustrator file, you'll sacrifice detail, so the key is to bring Illustrator files into Photoshop at exactly the right size. If simply using the Show Rulers command isn't exacting enough, in Photoshop, first measure the space into which you'll place an Illustrator file. Open the Info Palette, then choose your Line tool, set the minimum opacity (1%) and, with the Shift key down, click and drag from the start to the end location. While doing this, note the value in the Info palette representing the horizontal or vertical distance you just measured. In Illustrator, select the object you want to move into Photoshop and resize it to fit the space you just measured by using the Scale To Dimension filter included on the *Wow!* disk, or by calculating the scale percentage, or resizing "proxy boxes" to determine the correct scaling percentages (see Tip on top of page 13), making certain the "Scale line weight" option is enabled.

Monroy's preferred method is to prescale and copy his Illustrator file, and from within Photoshop, select the area into which he wants to paste and then choose Edit: Paste Into. He can move the Illustrator image around within that selected area, then deselect it to make it part of the main image or put it into its own layer.

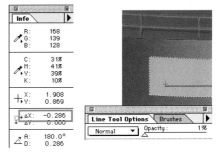

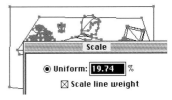

An Illustrator image; next measuring the space for pasting from within Photoshop; then scaling the image to the right size in Illustrator

After selecting an area, using Paste Into to place the copied Illustrator image within the selection

In addition to using Illustrator (to create details) and Photoshop (for retouching), sometimes Monroy brings 3D elements (he doesn't use photos) rendered in RayDream Designer (see pages 187–188) to help him visualize large objects, such as buildings, from different angles

MONROY

©Bert Monroy 1994

  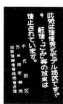  

Gallery (with Photoshop): Bert Monroy

Bert Monroy constructed this image by placing and retouching Illustrator objects in Photoshop (see pages 176–177). Illustrator enabled Monroy to work with perspective lines (page 96), create micro-fine lines (such as the bicycle spokes), maintain letter-form details, and make quick, local-color changes.

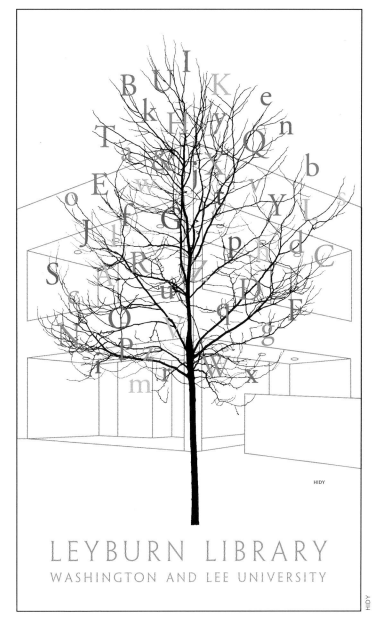

Gallery (with Photoshop): Lance Hidy

Lance Hidy began this illustration by scanning a photo of the Leyburn Library into Photoshop. After days of painstakingly isolating the tree from the background, Hidy used Levels to establish a "threshold" determining which pixels would be black and which would be white. He then converted this tree (still technically grayscale) to bitmap and saved it as an EPS using the "Transparent whites" option (page 84). In Illustrator, Hidy traced the building (using a scanned pencil tracing as a template; see page 80 for more on templates) and then placed the EPS tree. Hidy added Point-Type elements (which he distributed randomly,) for the alphabet and used Area Type for the title (see Chapter 7).

Gallery (with Photoshop):
Pamela Drury Wattenmaker

Pamela Drury Wattenmaker initially created the microscope in Illustrator. In Photoshop, she then rasterized a version of the microscope without the type and saved it in EPS format. Drury Wattenmaker then placed the EPS back into Illustrator where she masked it with a rectangle placed on top of it (see Chapter 8 for more on masks). She then cut this masked EPS, selected the type and "frame" and Pasted In Back (⌘-B) the masked EPS to go behind the frame and type, yet in front of everything else.

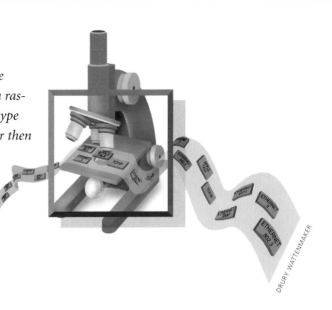

DRURY WATTENMAKER

Gallery (with Photoshop):
Michael Kline / Acme Design

Michael Kline began this image in two separate Illustrator files: one for the background, and another for the "rays." He opened each in Photoshop at the exact same size and resolution so he could use Calculate: Duplicate to load the "rays" as a selection in the background. He then "feathered" the selection 3 pixels and used Brightness/Contrast to "ghost it back." Lastly, Kline saved the composite background as an EPS and placed it back into Illustrator, where he added the airplanes and type.

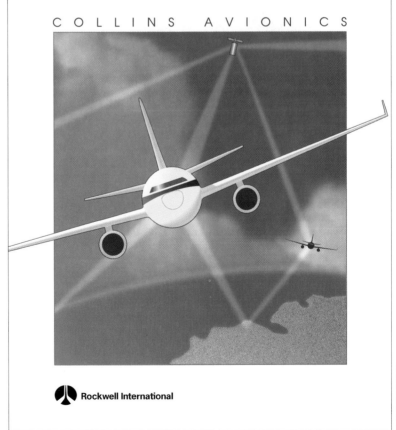

KLINE/ACME DESIGN

MORRIS (illustration), STOREY (photography) / SAN FRANCISCO EXAMINER

Gallery (with Photoshop): Chris Morris / *San Francisco Examiner*

For an article discussing issues of copyright protection with the advent of digital imaging, Chris Morris created an illustration using black, enclosed, flat-colored objects in Illustrator. Where he wanted eventually to place photographs, Morris created black-stroked, white objects as placeholders. Morris opened the Illustrator image in Photoshop, then from another file, he selected and copied a scanned photo of Peter Gabriel, shot by Examiner *photographer John Storey. In the main rasterized image, he used the Magic-wand tool to select the first placeholder for the photo and chose Edit: Paste Into. While the selection was still active, Morris used Image: Effects (Scale, Skew, Perspective and Distort) to fit the photo properly within the selected space before he "stamped it down." Morris repeated this procedure for each image he wished to place. (**Hint:** In Illustrator, try using colors not used anywhere in your image as placeholders, making it simple to pick up these colors with the Magic-wand within Photoshop.)*

Gallery (with Streamline): Lance Jackson/ *San Francisco Examiner*

To achieve the hard-edged, yet warm, painterly Illustrator look in this image, Lance Jackson sketched with traditional drawing media, then scanned the drawings into the computer at both high and low resolutions. In Streamline, Jackson translated both resolutions into Illustrator format. Opening the two translated files in Illustrator, Jackson combined them, using primarily the lower-resolution version while copying and pasting details from the higher-resolution version (the face and hands, for example). Finally, Jackson selected and recolored individual objects until he achieved the final effect in this illustration entitled "Doper."

SPOLLEN

Gallery (with Streamline): Christopher Spollen

Although his illustrations have the feel of bitmapped images, Chris Spollen creates them with Illustrator and Streamline. Spollen has developed a way of working with the computer that borrows from his traditional printmaking background. Beginning with scans of old magazines, and sketches of his own, Spollen runs these images through Streamline. Opening the files in Illustrator, he prints them out, and then physically cuts and pastes the printouts, rescans the resulting collages, and reruns the new scans through Streamline. Sometimes Spollen's files go through many "states" before he finally incorporates color into the image; often he reworks a piece using original drawings in Illustrator.

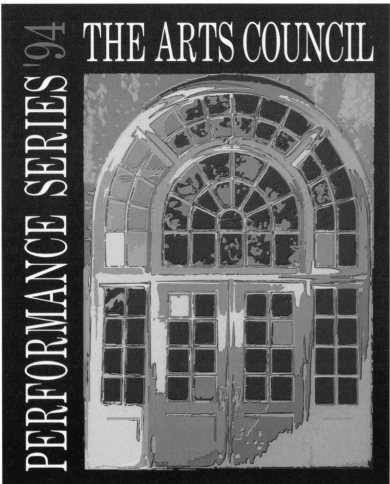

Gallery (with Streamline): Vince DiFabritus / Procter & Gamble

For this poster, Vince DiFabritus scanned the photo at the right, and opened it in Streamline where he set the Color/Grayscale Setup option to a Posterization of 26 colors. DiFabritus then opened the posterized file in Illustrator, and, because Streamline creates custom colors (instead of process colors), he was able to double-click on a color name in the Paint Style palette, and make adjustments to the colors Streamline had generated. As he adjusted the color recipes of some of the colors slightly, while redefining others completely with TruMatch colors, Illustrator automatically updated the image (see Chapter 3 *for more on Custom Colors).*

STEUER

Gallery (with Painter/Photoshop): Sharon Steuer

I originally created this image for a Computer Graphics World *review of Illustrator 5. I painted the landscape in Photoshop and Painter, and used Painter's Lighting Effects (see* The Painter Wow! Book *for details). After placing the landscape (as an EPS) into the Illustrator composition, I determined how to space the window panes and Option-double-clicked on the landscape to reopen it in Photoshop. I then created and activated a "selection mask" of the window leading (offset slightly) and painted shadows within the selection using the Burn tool. Also in Photoshop, I retouched (with sepia tones) a scanned photo of my grandmother and then, with the Oval-selection tool, I made a selection that framed the portrait. From the Paths palette, I converted the selection to a path, saved the path (naming it "oval"), and chose the Clipping Path option from the palette to define "oval" as a clipping path. In order for the shape of the portrait to actually be "clipped" by the oval (once it was placed in Illustrator), I saved the portrait as an EPS, choosing "oval" as the clipping path. I also saved a small, low-resolution PICT landscape (1" wide at 72 ppi) in Photoshop, which I opened from within Illustrator by choosing Filter: Create: Mosaic. I then grouped the mosaic, and chose Filter: Distort: Free Distort to create the picture on the table.*

STAHL

Gallery (with Painter/Photoshop): Nancy Stahl

*When Nancy Stahl decided to rework the portrait of the woman from her
"Couple in the Field" (page 89), she rasterized and cropped the portrait in
Photoshop. Next, Stahl both opened the rasterized image in Painter and imported Illustrator paths as friskets. Using the friskets allowed her to isolate
distinct areas of the image for local painting and retouching, and for apply-*

*ing specific effects, such as lighting
and texture. (**Hint:** Before importing
paths as friskets, Stahl now uses the
Pathfinder: Merge filter on a copy of
the image to eliminate path overlaps;
for more on filters, see* Chapter 6.*)*

Gallery (with RayDream Designer / Photoshop):
Wendy Grossman

Wendy Grossman began her illustration "The Bicycle Race" by drawing a tight pencil sketch, which she scanned and saved as a PICT so she could open it as a template in Illustrator (see page 80 for more on templates). Using the template, Grossman created the main composition in Illustrator. She constructed and rendered the flowers and the shrubs in RayDream Designer, giving them the look of a pop-up collage. Then she rasterized the Illustrator file in Photoshop, where she assembled all of the RayDream Designer vegetation and reworked the entire image using the painting and retouching tools.

The Traveling Radio Show™

Goes to Seattle!

The Traveling Radio Show™
"Serious nonsense since 1975"

STEUER

Gallery (with RayDream Designer/Photoshop): Sharon Steuer

*Illustrator was the starting point for this cassette-tape liner (called a "J-card"). The first task I performed in Illustrator was to create separate outlines for each portion of the radio logo (with the Pen tool). Saving each radio outline in Illustrator 3 format, I imported them into RayDream Designer, where I gave each depth and texture, assembled all the radio objects, and rendered them as a PICT file with a mask. Back in Illustrator, relying on source photos for rough visual references, I used the Pen tool to draw the Seattle skyline and the "Space Needle" directly in Illustrator. To establish the overall color scheme, I created gradients and used the Gradient-fill tool to specify their length and direction (see Chapter 5 for more on gradients). I created trim marks by placing an unfilled, unstroked rectangle the size of the final trim and choosing Filter: Create: Trim Marks. I then made the different type objects, rotated the "Goes to Seattle!" line and saved each type object into a separate Illustrator file. In Photoshop, I rasterized, retouched and color-corrected the skyline (see page 176 for more on rasterizing). I then brought each line of type into its own channel, loaded it as a selection and filled it, or, in the case of the drop shadow, offset and darkened it using Levels. Finally, I copied the masked radio and pasted it into place to complete the illustration. (**Hint:** Try pasting type as paths into Photoshop.)*

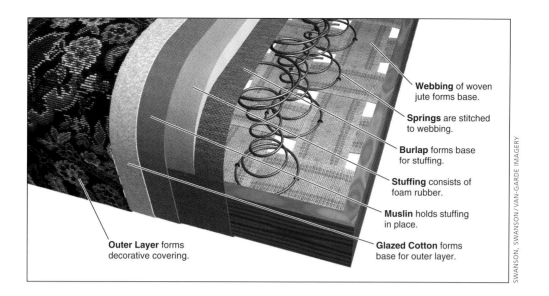

Webbing of woven jute forms base.

Springs are stitched to webbing.

Burlap forms base for stuffing.

Stuffing consists of foam rubber.

Muslin holds stuffing in place.

Glazed Cotton forms base for outer layer.

Outer Layer forms decorative covering.

SWANSON, SWANSON/VAN-GARDE IMAGERY

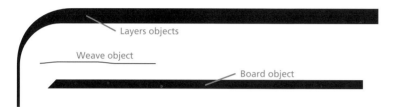

Layers objects

Weave object

Board object

Gallery (with StudioPro/Photoshop): Dan and Darlene Swanson

For Dan and Darlene Swanson, the first step in constructing realistic 3D renderings is to create accurate profiles of cross-sections in Illustrator. For the upholstery illustration above, the profiles for the various layers of fabric and foam were drawn in exactly the correct positions and sizes in relation to each other. The Swansons imported these profiles into Studio-Pro where they extruded them into the appropriate thicknesses and rotated them into the correct positions. They constructed the interwoven straps by creating a single modular "weave"

object, which they replicated and moved to form the "woofs" and "warps." They turned and duplicated the "board" object so the mitered corners would fit together. Texture maps, previously created in Photo-shop, were then assigned to each layer, lights were directed into the assembled scene, and the full image was rendered in PICT format. The Swansons lightly retouched the final rendered upholstery image in Photoshop, saved it in EPS format and placed it back into Illustrator, where they added the labels and border. The glass award (above right) required a bit more retouching in Photoshop, namely a few extra highlights painted on the edges, and some reworking of the type.

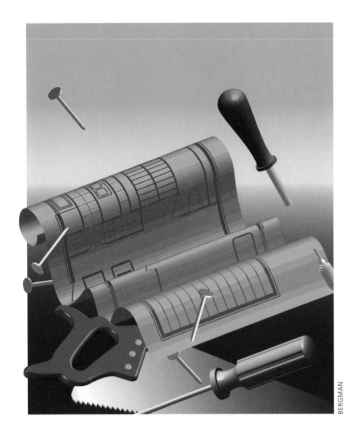

Nail

Screwdriver

Blueprint profile

Gallery (with Dimensions): Eliot Bergman

*Eliot Bergman used a combination of Illustrator and Dimensions
to create this "Blueprint for Savings." Bergman began in Illustrator
where he drew the flat views of each object, using many filters to help
him along (for the handle of the saw, for instance, he used the Pathfinder: Unite filter to combine basic objects, followed by the Stylize:
Round Corners filter). Sometimes Bergman drew only one view of
the object; at other times he needed to draw multiple views. For objects such as the saw, Bergman drew one side view only. In Dimensions he extruded the handle using the "Tall-Round" bevel, while
giving the blade no bevel (the extrusion for the blade was much thinner than the handle). For the
screwdriver, he drew half of the side view (revolving it around its profile) and the top rounded cap. The
nails were also drawn in half-side view and revolved around their profiles. Bergman drew the blueprint
full-front and converted the lines to filled objects using Filter: Objects: Outline Path (see Chapter 6 for
more on filters). He drew another separate path with the Pen tool to define the profile view of the
rolling blueprint. Although he formed and angled all objects independently in Dimensions, in order to
avoid the excess objects that Dimensions generates when computing lighting, Bergman designed most of
the lighting effects by using gradients as he assembled the separate objects in Illustrator.*

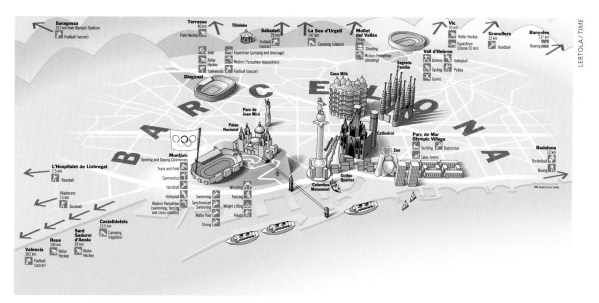

LERTOLA / *TIME*

Gallery (with Dimensions): Joseph Lertola / *Time*

Joseph Lertola designed this map of the venues at the Barcelona Olympics using Illustrator. He drew an aerial view of only the roads and shoreline, converted the lines to filled objects using Filter: Objects: Outline Path (see Chapter 6 *for more on filters), and then brought this aerial view into Dimensions where he angled it back, gave it a small thickness and curved it slightly. Once he achieved this receding perspective, Lertola brought the aerial view back into Illustrator and recombined it with the detailed buildings and assorted icons representing the various events.*

MAGLIARI / WORLD WRESTLING FEDERATION

Gallery (with traditional airbrush): Paul Magliari / World Wrestling Federation

Large billboards present unique challenges. Since Illustrator files don't decrease in resolution as they are enlarged, Illustrator could be considered the ideal design environment for the variable size reproduction needs of billboard creation. Paul Magliari began the illustration above by tracing over detailed skyline templates (see Chapter 4 *for more on templates) and used custom blends to create subtle changes in color. The World Wrestling Federation then composited the skyline with a traditional airbrush illustration to form the billboard shown above right.*

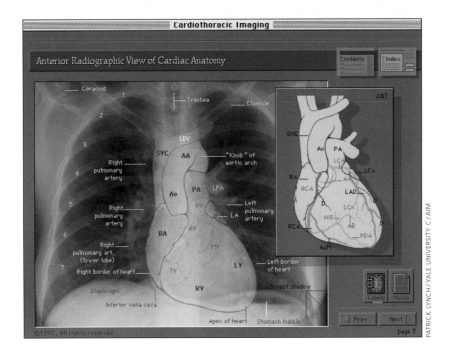

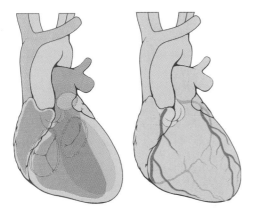

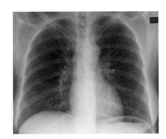

Gallery (with SuperCard/Photoshop): Patrick Lynch/Yale University C/AIM

Patrick Lynch uses Illustrator to create the base illustrations for his interactive CD-ROM development, then uses the Place command from within Photoshop to turn the illustrations into bitmaps. This technique allows him to rasterize fine-lined Illustrator images in much greater detail than would be possible in Photoshop alone (see page 176). As a medical illustrator, Lynch uses Illustrator to create detailing in anatomical diagrams, which he can easily adapt by changing colors, adding or subtracting elements, resizing and reshaping, or even overlaying these Illustrator illustrations on top of actual medical films and imaging. For the heart screen above, Lynch rasterized a version of the heart in Photoshop at exactly the correct size and resolution (it had to be scaled slightly horizontally in Illustrator first), and then transparently combined the heart with a scan of an actual chest X-ray. He then brought the individual renderings into SuperCard, where he implemented full interactivity and animation.

Gallery (with modems / QuarkXPress): Dan Cosgrove *(illustration)*, **David Fridberg** *(design)*

For a poster announcing the Smithsonian Institution's 1994 Jazz Orchestra Series, David Fridberg commissioned Dan Cosgrove to create the original illustration. The only problem was this: Fridberg lives in Washington, DC, and Cosgrove lives in Chicago, and the schedule was too tight to allow for even overnight mail deliveries. Illustrator's small file size (compared to Photoshop, for instance) made sending the working versions of the files via modem quick and easy. Cosgrove created rough sketches directly in Illustrator, then "modemed" them to Fridberg to comment on. With immediate

*feedback, Cosgrove was able to complete the illustration for the poster in record time. Since he knew that Fridberg would be pulling out individual musicians from the full composition, Cosgrove created each musician in his own layer, making it simple for Fridberg to select and copy any of them by hiding and showing the appropriate layers (see Chapter 4 for more on layers). With the final illustration received in DC, Fridberg used a combination of Illustrator and QuarkXPress to complete the design for this two-sided, fold-out poster. He created all graphic text (titles and the text on a curve) in Illustrator, although he decided to assemble the full poster from within QuarkXPress. (**Hint:** Since this Wow! book is produced in QuarkXPress, in order to fit the large (14"x20") poster onto this page, I used the File: Save Page as EPS option, then resized the placed page in QuarkXPress.)*

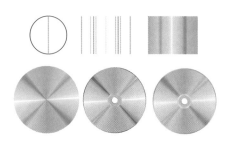

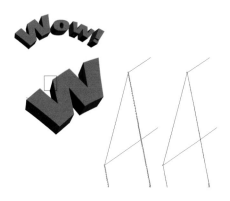

Gallery: (with QuarkXPress / Photoshop)

Barbara Sudick *(design)* / **Sharon Steuer** *(illustration)*

For The Illustrator 6 Wow! Book *back cover, typography designed by Barbara in a QuarkXPress page was saved as an EPS and opened directly in Illustrator. For the front cover, I began with embedded image objects for the sky background and the inner sky, then substituted linked EPS versions for printing (so I could re-modem individual elements if necessary). The inner sky was masked by a palette drawn with the Pen tool (the hole was cut out using Compound Path—see* Chapter 8, *page 154). In order to filter only selected portions of the background, filters had to be applied in Photoshop (see ⑥). The CD-ROM illustration was created by adapting a technique discovered by Bill Snebold: Blends can be applied around a circle using Path Patterns! After determining that the height of one blend object should be equal to the diameter of the circle, I created a multi-object blend, selected the blend and chose Object: Pattern to create it as a New pattern. Selecting the circle, I chose Filter: Stylize: Path Pattern, loaded the new pattern into "Sides" and clicked OK. After adding more details and a compound mask to cut the hole, I chose Object: Rasterize in RGB, and since rasterized objects have rectangular boundaries, I chose the Mask option. After applying Filter: Blur: Radial Blur with a Spin of 5, I re-rasterized the CD to convert it to CMYK. In the first edition of the book, the "Wow!" type began as Path Type on a curve, was converted to outlines, transformed using a Letraset Envelopes filter, then adjusted manually with the Direct-selection tool. For this edition, I used the KPT Vector Effects: 3D Transform filter on the "Wow!" then eliminated the hundreds of extra anchor points generated by the 3D filter with BeInfinite's Smart Remove Points. (See the* Wow! *disk's Plug-ins folder for a free copy of BeInfinite's Smart Remove Points, and demos of Letraset's Envelopes and KPT Vector Effects.)*

The
Illustrator 6

Adobe Illustrator 6 Tryout!

Macintosh
WOW! CD!
Included

Plug-ins and filters, FREE clip-art, and more!

WOW!

Book

Sharon Steuer

Step-by-Step

Techniques, Tips & Tricks from 80 Leading Illustrator Artists

SUDICK (design) / STEUER (illustration)

Technical Notes

Book Design

Barbara Sudick is the artist behind the *Illustrator Wow!* design and typography. Using Jill Davis's layout of *The Photoshop Wow! Book* as a jumping-off point, she designed the pages in QuarkXPress, using Adobe fonts Frutiger and Minion, and, on the front cover, Mistral and Univers.

Hardware and Software

My primary computer configuration was a Macintosh Quadra 700, with 64 MB of RAM, an APS 1.3 MB external drive, an Apple CD-ROM drive, a 44 MB SyQuest drive, SupraFax/Modem, and an APS Archive Python DAT backup using Dantz's Retrospect archiving software. Color proofs of first edition were made on a Tektronix Phaser 300i printer, with proofs of the cover on an Iris printer. TIFF Export (Vision's Edge) created thumbnails for the Peachpit website. On the road, I used a Powerbook 160 and an APS faxmodem so I could keep in touch with the *Wow!* testers.

For software, in addition to Adobe Illustrator: Adobe Photoshop, QuarkXPress, XPert Tools II (ALAP), QuicKeys (CE Software), Capture (Mainstay), Arcane's "Scale To Dimension" filter (on the *Wow!* disk in the Plug-ins folder) and Dantz's Retrospect for archiving. I communicated with testers using Claris Emailer and klunky America Online, sending pages in Acrobat PDF format. I also used Day-to-Day Contacts (Day-to-Day Software), and Aladdin's Stuffit/Installermaker.

Pre-press (Color Separations and Proofs)

High Resolution, Inc., based in midcoast Maine, led by Peter Koons and Sandy Soards, produced the color-separated composite film and final color proofs for this book and for its cover. The photos in the book were drum-scanned on an Optronics ColorGetter and imported using Kodak Precision Color Management. Many illustrations were trapped using Island Trapper (Island Graphics Corporation). Screen captures were separated in Photoshop 3 using a GCR with maximum black generation. To track updated placed files and convert spot colors within illustrations, HighRes used PictAttributes (Markware), and Spot (ALAP), respectively. Individual pages were spooled through Helios Ethershare to a Sun Microsystems Sparc Workstation, swapping FPO scans for full resolution images via OPI as served by Kodak Prophecy. Pages were rasterized by Adobe PostScript RIPs and output using Panther imagesetting technology employing ESCOR screening from Prepress Solutions. Color proofs of each page were made using the Kodak Contract proofing system.

How to contact the author...

Sharon Steuer, c/o Peachpit Press, 2414 Sixth Street, Berkeley, CA 94710, or via Internet e-mail: *WowArtist@aol.com*, or via the Web: *http://www.peachpit.com/meetus/authors/sharon.steuer.html*

Acknowledgments

First thanks must go to Linnea Dayton (the *Wow!* series editor) and to Peachpit's Ted Nace. Thanks too, to *The Photoshop Wow! Book* authors, and to the entire Peachpit staff.

My most heartfelt gratitude goes to the more than 70 artists and Illustrator experts who generously allowed me to include their work and divulge their techniques.

Special thanks to Patricia Pane for believing in this project, and being instrumental in making it happen. Sonya Schaffer, Liz Bulger, Sandra Glaser, Ellen Ablow and Sean McKenna were also of invaluable help. Thanks also to the entire team of Adobe Illustrator engineers and technicians.

I have had the tremendous fortune to work with a magnificent team on this project. Barbara Sudick expertly designed the layout of this book. Mordy Golding co-authored the Illustrator 6 revisions. Gary Pfitzer has been a brilliant and meticulous editor. Peg Maskell Korn and Brenda Brody tirelessly proofed the manuscript. Sincere gratitude goes to my stellar team of testers and consultants: Eve Elberg, Joanne Chernow, Mary Littell, Simone Weissman and Terry Sisk Graybill. Sandee Cohen continues to be the best Illustrator cohort and consultant that I could possibly imagine. Michelle Rosemary Simpson was the innovative *Wow!* indexer. Peg metamorphosed into my personal and production assistant—without whom this project would not have seen completion.

Curating the artwork in this book was an immense job in itself, and it couldn't have been done without the generous networking help of: Adobe's Luanne Cohen and Colleen Muller, Clay Andres, Telitha Harper (Step-by-Step Electronic Design) and Linnea Dayton. Also, thanks to Laurie Grace, Lori Barra, Tom Cushwa, Chris Cave, Pepe Moreno, Bert Monroy, and Cher Threinen-Pendarvis.

Peggy Kilburn schedules the Macworld *Illustrator Wow! Artists* conferences. Tom McMillan and *Computer Artist Magazine* prints excerpts from this book. Tim Debaets, Tim Nighswander and the incomparable Howard Brody also lent their expertise.

Thanks to: A.J. Rogers, with Jennifer Jones and Sally Lampe (Tektronix), Peter Alpers (Iris), Kenny Sagnelli (Planetwide Productions). APS Peripherals, Aladdin Software, ALAP, and Dantz. Thanks also to the Adobe Type department, BeInfinite, Letraset, Extensis, Cytopia, Alien Skin, Dynamic Graphics, Aridi, MapArt, MetaTools, Image Club Graphics, Ultimate Symbol, Intrepid, Chronchart, Arcane and Design Tools Monthly for their special *Wow!* offers.

High Resolution Inc. (Peter Koons, Sandy Soards, Shawna Elwell, Chris Cunningham and John Higgins), a phenomenal prepress facilitiy in midcoast Maine, expertly produced *all* the PostScript color separations for this book. High Resolution wishes to thank: Island Graphics (Jeff Guns and Mark Alan Cirino), and PrePRESS Solutions (Bob Trenkamp and Irene Schrader).

Artists

⑥ Full listing of these artists is in
"What's New?" on the *Wow!* disk.

Resources

Adobe Systems, Inc.
1585 Charleston Rd.
P.O. Box 7900
Mountainview, CA 94039
800-833-6687
http://www@adobe.com/

AGFA
200 Ballardvale Street
MS 200-4-9-B
Willmington, MA 01887
508-658-5600 x5170

Aladdin Systems, Inc. *Stuffit*
165 Westridge Drive
Watsonville, CA 95076-4159
408-761-6200

ALAP *XPert Tools*
see XChange

Alien Skin Software, LLC *Plug-ins*
800 St. Mary's Street/Suite 100
Raleigh, NC 27605-1457
919-832-4124

Allegiant Technologies *SuperCard*
9740 Scranton Road/Suite 300
San Diego, CA 92121
619-587-0500

America Online
800-827-6364

Apple Computer
800-767-2775

APS Technologies *Hardware*
6131 Deramus/P.O. Box 4987
Kansas City, MO 64120-0087
800-874-1427

Arcane *Scale To Dimension Filter*
1240 San Thomas Aquino
Suite 101
San José, CA 95117

Aridi Computer Graphics *Digital Art*
P.O. Box 797702
Dallas, TX 75379
214-404-9171

BeInfinite, Inc. *InfiniteFX Filters*
4651 Woodstock Rd./
Suite 203, #210
Roswell, GA 30075-1686
404-552-6624

Cartesia Software *MapArt Designer*
5 South Main Street/P.O. Box 757
Lambertville, NJ 08530
800-334-4291

CE Software, Inc. *QuicKeys*
P.O. Box 65580
West Des Moines, IA 50265
515-221-1801

Chronchart
4640 Edgewood Ave.
Oakland, CA 94602
510-482-3576

Claris Corp. *Emailer*
Santa Clara CA
800-544-8554/408-987-7000

Cytopia Software Inc. *Socket Set*
1735 E. Bayshore Road/Suite 30b
Redwood City, CA 94063
415-364-4594

Dantz *Retrospect*
4 Orinda Way/Bldg C
Orinda, CA 94563
510-253-3000

Day-to-Day Software *Contacts*
244 Westchester Avenue/Suite 310
White Plains, NY 10604
800-329-8632
914-686-1018

Dynamic Graphics Inc. *Clip art, etc.*
6000 N. Forest Pk. Drive
Peoria, IL 61614
800-255-8800

Extensis Corporation *Draw Tools*
55 S.W. Yamhill Street/Fourth Fl.
Portland, OR 97204
800-796-9798/503-274-2020

Fractal Design Corp. *Painter*
335 Spreckels Drive/Suite F
Aptos, CA 95003
408-688-8800

Goodies/Bruce Bowman
1344 Fairway Entrance Dr.
San José, CA 95131
http://www.iriesoft.com/

High Resolution, Inc.
87 Elm Street
Camden, ME 04843-1941
207-236-3777

Intrepid *Sree Kotay's SCT Inset Path*
1706 Diamond Drive
Newton, PA 18940
215-579-9474

IRIS Graphics, Inc.
Six Crosby Drive
Bedford, MA 01730
617-275-8777

Island Graphics Corp. *IslandTrapper*
4000 Civic Center Drive
San Rafael, CA 94903
415-491-1000

Sree Kotay *see* Intrepid Systems

Letraset
40 Eisenhower Drive
Paramus, NJ 07653
800-343-8973 x7210
800-634-3463

Macromedia *FreeHand*
600 Townsend Street
San Francisco, CA 94103
800-989-3762

Mainstay *Capture*
591-A Constitution Ave.
Camarillo, CA 93012
805-484-9400

MetaTools, Inc.. *Vector Effects*
6303 Carpinteria Avenue
Carpinteria, CA 93013
805-566-6200

Microsoft Corp. *Excel*
One Microsoft Way
Redmond, WA 98052
206-882-8080

Pantone, Inc.
590 Commerce Blvd.
Carlstadt, NJ 07072
201-935-5500

Peachpit Press
2414 Sixth Street
Berkeley, CA 94710
800-283-9444 / 510-548-4393

Planetwide Productions, Inc.
652 Glenbrook Road
Stamford, CT 06906
203-967-8808

PrePRESS Solutions *Panther*
11 Mount Pleasant Avenue
East Hanover, NJ 07936
800-443-6600

Quark, Inc. *QuarkXPress*
Denver, CO
800-788-7835

RayDream *RayDream Designer*
1804 N. Shoreline Blvd.
Mountain View, CA 94103
800-846-0111/415-960-1198

Strata, Inc. *StudioPro*
2 West St.George Blvd./Suite 2100
St. George, UT 84770
800-787-2823/801-628-9756

Tektronix Inc.
26600 SW Parkway
Wilsonville, OR 97070
800-835-6100

TruMatch, Inc.
331 Madison Ave.
New York, NY 10017
212-351-2360

Ultimate Symbol *Design Elements*
31 Wildertness Drive
Stony Point, NY 10980
914-942-0003

Vision's Edge *TIFF Export*
3491-11 Thomasville Rd./Ste 177
Tallahassee, FL 32308
800-983-6337
904-386-4573

WACOM *ArtZ Tablet*
115 Century Road
Paramus, NJ 07652
800-922-6613

XChange *XTensions for QuarkXPress*
P.O. Box 270578
Ft. Collins, CO 80527
800-788-7557

Publications

Adobe Press Books/Hayden Books
Macmillan Computer Publishing
Indianapolis, IN
800-428-5331
Design/Production Essentials
Imaging Essentials
Illustrator Classroom in a Book

Design Tools Monthly
Boulder, CO
303-444-6876

IDG Books Worlwide, Inc.
San Mateo, CA
415-312-0650
Macworld Illustrator 6 Bible
by Ted Alspach

Peachpit Press
Berkeley, CA
800-283-9444 / 510-548-4393
The Illustator 6 Book
by Deke McClelland
Illustrator 6 for Macintosh
Visual Quickstart Guide
by Elaine Weinmann & Peter
Lourekas
Illustrator Illuminated, 2nd ed.
by Clay Andres
The Painter Wow! Book
by Cher Threinen-Pendarvis
The Photoshop Wow! Book
by Linnea Dayton & Jack Davis
The Smiley Dictionary
by Seth Godin

Penwell Publishing Company
Computer Artist Magazine
Computer Graphics World
Nashua, NH
800-225-0556

Random House
New York
Illustrator Filter Finesse
Ted Alspach & Jennifer Alspach

Step-by-Step Publications
Step-by-Step Electronic Design
Peoria, IL
800-255-8800/309-688-8866

Yale University Press
New Haven, CT
203-432-0948
Manual of Ornithology
by Patrick Lynch & Noble Proctor
The Shape of Time
by George Kubler

General Index

techniques *(continued)*
organizing; overprinting; posterizing; printing; program interactions; proofing; rasterizing; reducing; rendering; reordering; resizing; rotating; saving; scaling; scanning; selecting; sketching; tracing; transformations; trapping; troubleshooting; unlocking
effects, *see* brush strokes; collages; lighting effects; painterly images; perspective; repeating patterns; resolution; special effects
templates 77–98, 130
   see also techniques
   digitizing logos with 80
   (gallery) 53, 186
   graphs use as 12
   PICTs opened as 23
   preparing 80–81
   quick opening 80
   techniques with 52, 68, 80–81, 96–98, 130–131
   tracing 81
      relief with 82
text
   see also type
   filters 136–137
   objects 136
textures *see* Ink Pen; Path Patterns; patterns
Thomas•Bradley Illustration & Design 112–113, 122, 162–163
TIFF files
   see also file(s), formats, ⑥
   importing 22
TIFF image, importing 21, 22, ⑥
   coloring 1-bit 22
   see also formats
tiles
   Transform pattern tiles 74
   in Path Patterns 129
Time magazine 101, 102–103, 156, 191
Tinkel, Kathleen 5, 126, 128, 138
tints
   with Colors filters 128
   filling objects with 51
   of colors 62, 64
   with Pathfinder Soft/Hard filters 121
   specifying percentages 62
   tint slider 51
toggles
   see also Glossary inside back cover; tools
   palette underlines 15
Toolbox *see* individual tool names
tools

see also elements; menus; palettes; techniques; under individual tool names
basic, exercises in using 41
mastering techniques 27
   see also filters
Toyo
   CMYK process color models 65
tracing
   see also layers; templates
   geometric tool use 83
   reliefs 82
   scanned art 68
   Streamline use for 175
   as technique for coloring line drawings 85, 95
   template 81
   true horizontals and verticals 98
tracking 134, 135
training iii
Training folder Wow! disk
Transform each 125
transforming 13–14
   see also copying; creating; deleting; editing; moving; reflecting; rotating; scaling; skewing
   combining 64, 83, 162, 167, 172
   gradients into masked blends 159
   patterns 74
   perspective lines into guides 97
   power 13
   reflecting 13, 41, 172
   resizing, line weight and 174
   rotating 13
      comp 187
      documents 26
      lesson 38–39
   scaling
      for placement in other programs 174
      lesson 38–39, 41
      line weights 174
      objects 13
      Page Setup options for 19
      patterns 74
      Scale-line-weight enabling 81, 174
      smooth blend use 113
   stretching 57
   tools for 13–14
   views 57
transparencies
   with colors and masks 157
   cropping as technique for 131
   cut-away 166
   with filters 51, 122, 130–131, 132, 172
   glowing 165
   with value 51
   X-ray 192
transparent whites
   saving EPS images with 85, 95, 179

trees, creating 168
Transform Each (Arrange menu) 125
Trap (Pathfinder) filter 21
trapping 21, 55, 64
   see also printing; techniques
trim marks 146, 147
   Trim Marks (Create) filter 126, 147, 188
Trim (Pathfinder) filter 121
troubleshooting
   avoiding common mistakes 6, 14, 16
   banding in on screen illustrations 114
   color consistency 65, 67
   custom colors, filter and gradient problems 128
   exported files
      white rectangle problems 152
      into Photoshop 25
   filters, text wrap problems 135
   fonts, missing 136
   gradients, conversion to blends by Illustrator 3.2 format 25
   graphs 11, 13
   grouping problems 9
   guides, grouping with objects 97
   training
      how to use this book iii
      recommendations iii
   joining 10
   locating stray points 119
   masks, unmasking objects not intended to be masked 153
   overlapping lines, differences between Artwork and Preview 49
   preventing problems
      archiving 16
      by backing up 16
      recommendations 4
      tool mastery as key to avoiding trouble (chapter) 27
   printing 24
      extraneous points 69
      mask problems 153
      proofing importance 24
      registration problems 64
      type converted to outlines 138
   proofing, importance of 24
   registration 66
   saving, when to use the Save As command 24
   scaling 26
   selection difficulties
      hidden edges as a cause 19
      problems with selecting objects 79
   setting Undos 17
   snapping-to-point 56
   styles
      new styles not being applied 14

Dedication

To my loving family and friends, who have continued to prop me up, and take care of me throughout this project, and who can now stop worrying for a while.

To my little Cassie-bear for keeping my chair warm during my confinement in the course of writing the first edition. And to her heirs apparent (Puma and Bear) for making me laugh again.

And of course, a most special dedication to Jeff Jacoby, my love and husband, who continues to prepare the delicious, gourmet, saturated-fat-free meals which feed the on-site *Wow!* staff…but mostly, for his unwavering love and belief in me.

The Illustrator 6 Wow! CD-ROM Disk Contents

Plus a few surprises!

"What's New in Illustrator 6?" folder & PDF:

- Onscreen-readable supplement in Acrobat PDF format with the latest Illustrator 6 tips, tricks, and step-by-step techniques
- Links to other Illustrator 6 related goodies

Adobe Illustrator 6 Tryout:

- For exploring and viewing Illustrator 6 work —even if you don't have Illustrator 6 yet!

And tryout versions, demos, and samples from major third-party plug-in developers:

- BeInfinite InfiniteFX
- Letraset Envelopes
- MetaTools KPT's Vector Effects
- Extensis Draw Tools
- Cytopia Socket Sets
- Alien Skin Stylist (with exclusive *Wow!* offer)

Plus these special *Wow!* filters:

- BeInfinite's Smart Remove Points
- Arcane's Scale To Dimension
- Sree Kotay's Inset Path
- Mike & Ted's Melt and Drip

Art, fonts, and samples from:

- Dynamic Graphics (clip art and more)
- Image Club (Mini Pics font and clip art)
- MapArt (Illustrator / TIFF format maps)
- Aridi (exquisite borders and letters)
- Ultimate Symbol (high quality symbols)

Training Folder:

- Zen Lessons
- Steuer & Cohen's "Glowing Light" mask lesson
- Eve Elberg's "Comet Gradient Lesson"
- FREE 3-day and 8-week course outlines using *The Illustrator 6 Wow! Book*

You asked for it...

Three **Advanced Techniques** masterworks on disk for you to pick apart and figure out:

- The Thomas•Bradley Racecar (*page 162*)
- Clarke Tate's "Mann's Theater" (*page 168*)
- Chris Morris's "Mafia Chef" (*page 161*)

Goodies including:

- Bruce Bowman's classic Illustrator Goodies (he defined the term!)
- Sandee Cohen's "Pixels in Illustrator"
- Victor von Salza's "Ink Pen Effects"
- Charts for Punk & Bloat and Scribble & Tweak filters by Randy Livingston
- Isometrics techniques by Dan Swanson, Kurt Hess and Steven Gordon

AI Chat News folder

Another source for tips and tricks—find out about the premier Illustrator online chat!

Publications—PDF excerpts from...

Graphics magazines and other Wow! books

Demos, samples and offers from all the programs shown in Chapter 9:

Adobe Photoshop/Streamline/Dimensions, Fractal Painter, Ray Dream Designer, Strata StudioPro, Allegiant SuperCard, QuarkXPress

More **Tips, Tricks, & Techniques revealed by the following *Wow!* Artists:**

Chris Burke, Rob Marquardt, K.D. Clark, Scott Crouse, Steven Gordon, Randy Zeitman, David Nelson, Kevin Barrack, Alan Weimer, Lester Yocum